PRAY FOR ME

....

STUDENT PRAYER GUIDE

THE STUDENT'S GUIDE TO BECOMING A PRAYER CHAMPION

TONY SOUDER

Tony Souder / LeaderTreks
25W560 Geneva Road, Suite 30
Carol Stream, IL 60188
PrayforMeCampaign.com

Pray for Me: Student Prayer Guide: A Student's Guide to Becoming a Prayer Champion/ Tony Souder

ISBN 978-0-9963750-1-6

CONTENTS

....

PART FOUR // PRAYING FOR THE LOST

FOREWORD

....

To Next Generation Leaders and the Church: I love what Tony Souder and the Pray for Me Campaign are doing. As someone who has devoted my life to the youth ministry movement I could not be more excited about how the Pray for Me Campaign is creating natural connections between adults and students through prayer. The idea that every young person in a church can have three adults from three different generations serve as their Prayer Champions each school year is ingenious. A little math reveals that a student could have 33 different adults as their Prayer Champions during their middle school, high school and college years. I like this! I want this for myself!

The focus on prayer really sets the campaign apart and gives any adult believer the opportunity to make a difference in the life of a young person. What better starting place for a true, deep connection between generations that will make a lasting difference in the lives of young people? My prayer is that churches everywhere would seriously consider making the Pray for Me Campaign a strategic part of how they minister to the next generation.

To Students: It seems that the longer I am in ministry the more I realize that no one succeeds on their own...no one. Whether you are a pastor, a parent, or a student, we all need other people who love and support us. We need a team of fans who are in our corner cheering us on in faith and life. I see young people all the time that are learning this lesson too late. The place in the bleachers where their cheering section is supposed to be is empty and they don't know what to do about it. One of the reasons I was willing to write this foreword was because the Pray for

Me Campaign provides students like you a simple way to help you fill the bleachers with adults and peers who care deeply about you succeeding in life, and it all starts with prayer.

My challenge for you as a student is to take advantage of both aspects of the Pray for Me Campaign! First, don't be afraid to invite adults to be your Prayer Champions for a school year. Even if your church hasn't officially launched the Pray for Me Campaign, it doesn't mean you can't go ahead and get started. Lead the way. I believe you will find adults more than willing to step up and serve you in this way. This may be one of the most important things you ever do to invest in your own future.

Secondly, gather a group of friends and commit to becoming Prayer Champions for each other by using this Prayer Guide. The book you are holding is designed just for that. As you and your peers pray for each other God will use these daily prayers to create an incredible bond between you. I am excited for every student who is able to experience the benefits of having a team of loving adults and peers who are committed to them in prayer and beyond.

Doug Fields
Author, Speaker, Youth Pastor
Co-Founder, Downloadyouthministry.com

TO THE NEXT GENERATION:

May the magnificence of Jesus capture your hearts daily!
May prayer become as natural and vital for you as breathing!
May you become relentlessly courageous for the cause of Christ!

SOUDER

Lord, teach us to pray

–LUKE 11:1

ACKNOWLEDGEMENTS

....

First, I want to thank my wife, Rhonda, who has been the difference maker in my life when it comes to understanding and experiencing lavish, passionate prayer. The sweetness of her enjoyment of our heavenly father in prayer is a beautiful thing to behold. My daughters, Abby and Bethany, are constant reminder that the next generation holds great promise for the cause of Christ!

Because this book is all about empowering students to be a supernatural force for the Kingdom of God through prayer, I want to give a special nod to all those who are called at some level to be champions for your generation, whether they are a Prayer Champion, parent, coach, teacher, or youth leader. Their role is vital and may their tribe increase.

Writing a book is hard work and for me it would be an impossible feat if it were not for the stellar team God has raised up to make it a reality. Thank you to all the gracious friends who read, reflected, and helped revise this book into a much better resource for the next generation. Specifically I am thankful for the in-house *Pray for Me* team: Lauren Gauthey, Hannah Johnson, Megan DeMoss, and Nathan Mileur. Thank you for your love for Jesus and your commitment to excellence.

Lastly, I want to thank all those who have made it possible for the Pray for Me Campaign to launch across the nation. You know who you are; you are our financial partners, board, and staff members, both past and present. Thank you for believing in the importance of mobilizing prayer for the next generation. May God be praised!

PREFACE

....

This Prayer Guide that you are holding is part of a larger movement of prayer called the Pray for Me Campaign. You may have heard of it. Your church may have already launched it or is launching right now and that is why you are reading this preface. Just in case you don't know anything about The Pray for Me Campaign, let me give you a brief heads up. The Pray for Me Campaign started as a way of establishing life-changing relationships between students like you and adults in the church through the catalyst of prayer. Students are equipped to invite three adults from three different generations to be their Prayer Champions for a school year. Each year students like you invite three new adults to be their Prayer Champions, creating an ever-growing team of adults who care for and support you. It's like building a fan base of people who are committed to cheering you on as you grow.

Several things became clear as the Pray for Me Campaign began launching in churches across the country. We found that the students were being greatly encouraged by their newfound connections within the church. We also found they were missing out on some of the goodness of having Prayer Champions! Too often students did not have a clear sense of the important things their Prayer Champions were praying for them because they did not have the Prayer Guide. Seeing this, we decided to create the Student Edition Prayer Guide to help students experience first hand the types of prayers that are being prayed for them by their Prayer Champions. It is one of my deepest prayers that God will use your engagement with this Prayer Guide to help you taste the sweetness of praying the Scriptures through the lens of The 7 Essentials for yourself and your peers.

INTRODUCTION

....

I was 17 when I accepted Christ as my Savior. I remember walking into church during those first few weeks after becoming a Christian. Adults repeatedly expressed their happiness for me, saying that they had been praying for me. As a newbie follower of Christ coming from a non-Christian home, I was clueless concerning the scope of what they were saying. When I reflect on what their prayers meant to me in those early days, several clear memories come to mind. First, I was amazed that I was even on the radar of any of these people. After all, I was essentially a stranger to them. I was also surprised that they would actually take the time to pray for me. I recall that surprise being quickly swallowed up by a strong sense of love and care from the adults. Their willingness to pray for me and their expressions of care and concern transformed the trajectory of my life. Though I was young, I did realize I had walked into a massive amount of goodness, and I liked it—a lot! The "goodness" that I had walked into was what the Bible calls the Body of Christ—the Church, a place filled with people who knew God and wanted me to know him. It seems that God loves to use the private and public prayers of his people to change the world, to change a teenager's world, like mine.

It is likely that you are holding this book because you care about your friends and have a desire for them to flourish. You may have been invited by someone as part of the Pray for Me Campaign to serve as a Prayer Champion for a friend or peer. Being a Prayer Champion is a simple way to provide significant spiritual impact and encouragement for those around you. This book exists to help you flourish in being a Prayer Champion for your friends. You may not feel like a Prayer Champion, but your willingness to dive into this Prayer Guide on behalf of others is affirmation that you are. This book will guide you in pursuing God's provision, protection, and purposes to be established in the lives of those you pray for. When we begin to pray like this for others, something amazing happens inside of us as well. Our hearts become larger toward God and others. We begin to move toward others to bless and encourage them in ways beyond prayer. This book is designed with that in mind.

My hope is that you will find uncontainable joy in praying Scripture over your generation. I also hope that you will respond with a resounding "Yes!" if and when God leads you to invest in their lives in other ways as well. It is my belief that a wave of God's goodness will follow the prayers of his people. With that in mind, may the goodness of God begin to flow freely because of your prayers!

The Golden Rule

How many times have you been asked to pray for someone only to forget about it later on? I would like to say that I have felt the full weight of every request when someone has asked me to pray for them, but that simply is not true. Regrettably, there have been times when I have not given the plea for prayer a second thought. Fortunately, my attentiveness to prayer was transformed one day when I was sitting in a hospital room after my wife's surgery in Long Island, New York. It wasn't like I was looking for transformation that day; I was minding my own business, reading through the Gospel of Matthew, when God opened my eyes to see a truth that in my blindness I had overlooked every other time I had read the familiar passage found in Matthew 7:7-12.

Ask and it will be given to you; seek, and you will find; knock, and it will be opened to you. For everyone who asks receives, and the one who seeks finds, and to the one who knocks it will be opened. Or which one of you, if his son asks him for bread, will give him a stone? Or if he asks for a fish, will give him a serpent? If you then, who are evil, know how to give good gifts to your children, how much more will your Father who is in heaven give good things to those who ask him!

I am very confident that you know the next verse, and yet you may be surprised to find it here in this context. It is the Golden Rule: "So whatever you wish that others would do to you, do also to them, for this is the Law and the Prophets" (Matthew 7:12).

Jesus put The Golden Rule right at the culminating point of a passage about deliberate, persistent, hopeful prayer. So here is my takeaway from that hospital room years ago: Jesus wants us to approach prayer for others with the same intensity and hopeful expectation as we would want them to approach praying for us. The Golden Rule can be used as a means to bring intensity and hopeful expectation to your prayers for others, especially your friends and peers who are in your neighborhood, church or school.

The Pray for Me Campaign is about hope, specifically the hope that you and others can find in the greatness of God. Every generation needs to find their greatest hope, satisfaction, and enjoyment in God. This campaign will help you lead your friends and peers to this hope through prayer. It is through prayer that the Holy Spirit sustains and strengthens our personal walk with God. This Prayer Guide is designed to help you and other followers of Christ like you call out to God for his loving provision, protection, and purposes in the lives of those in your generation. The Campaign has three aims for students:

1. Help each emerging generation see and savor the greatness of God through the prayers of God's people.

2. Help each emerging generation be empowered as Prayer Champions who intentionally pray for and invest in their generation.

3. Create a vast web of multi-generational relationships established by prayer, where each generation would share the greatness of God they have seen and savored with each other.

SEVEN WAYS TO USE THIS PRAYER GUIDE

....

1. We were created to live in community! Use this guide to pray for those in your small group, youth group, or other ministries like FCA, Young Life, CRU, Youth for Christ, RUF, etc.

2. Read the Introduction and Part One: The Adventure of Prayer to understand the purpose and format of this Prayer Guide.

3. Pray on your own for yourself, your friends, or perhaps even your siblings (pages 15 – 102).

4. Use this Prayer Guide to specifically pray for those who do not have a relationship with Christ (page 141).

5. Pray any day of the month using the 31-Day Cycle of Prayers (page 105).

6. Get to know and understand the 7 Essentials (page 4). They will help you flourish in your relationship with God and others.

7. Make seeing, savoring, and sharing the greatness of God a natural part of your relationship with him (page 5).

LET THE ADVENTURE

OF PRAYER

BEGIN!

PART ONE

....

THE ADVENTURE OF PRAYER

Welcome to the adventure of praying for your peers. Yes, I am using the word adventure concerning your prayers. Life with God is always an adventure and prayer is at the very heart of it. Prayer actually launches us into the adventure of having a relationship with God through Jesus. It is the first thing that anyone does as a follower of Jesus. In fact, you become a follower of Jesus by calling out to him for salvation in prayer. Prayer is clearly the visible starting point of our relationship with God, but it doesn't stop there. Prayer is our lifeline of ongoing relationship with Jesus. What an amazing gift God has given to us in prayer; to be able to have access to the King of the universe whenever or wherever we are is simply another example of his stunning and lavish grace!

Praying for someone to see and savor the truth of the Gospel is one of the most important and adventurous things you can ever do for them. It flows out of our relationship with Jesus and how we honor him with our lives. In this Prayer Guide you will be praying for yourself, close personal friends, and people you know only by name, but everyone you pray for matters. We *all* need people asking the King of the universe to bring his goodness to bear on our lives.

Praying the Scriptures

This guide is designed to give your prayers focus, clarity, and consistency through three primary components: praying the Scriptures, The 7 Essentials, and SeeSavorShare. We begin by establishing our roots in the truths of Scripture. The Bible is the Word of God and as such has the power to give life to us and our prayers. Throughout this book you will learn how to turn Scripture into prayers. Praying Scripture is one of the most powerful and authoritative ways to pray. Let's take a moment to be reminded of some of the promises that await us as we soak in the Scriptures.

The Word of God:
- Gives life (Psalm 119:25, 107)
- Strengthens (Psalm 119:28)
- Guards from sin and keeps us pure (Psalm 119:9, 11)
- Creates and sustains the universe (Psalm 33:6, 2 Peter 3:5, Hebrews 1:3, 11:3)
- Creates spiritual life (1 Peter 1:23, James 1:18)
- Is able to save our souls (James 1:21)
- Is living and active and able to discern the thoughts and intentions of the heart (Hebrews 4:12)
- Produces faith (Romans 10:17)
- Teaches, reproves, corrects, and trains in righteousness (2 Timothy 3:16)

These passages offer a taste of the goodness that flows from the supremacy and power of the Word of God.

One of the compelling aspects of this guide is that it takes the most powerful words in the world, the very words of God, and makes them the catalyst for our prayers. The apostle Paul in Ephesians 6:17 refers to the Scriptures as the "Sword of the Spirit," and we know from Hebrews 4:12 that "the word of God is living and active, sharper than any two-edged sword, piercing to the division of soul and of spirit, of joints and of marrow, and discerning the thoughts and intentions of the heart." God uses his Word to transform our hearts whether it is written, spoken, or uttered silently in prayer to the Father. In this Prayer Guide I am committed to letting the very truths of Scripture be the fuel for our prayers. We will take passages of Scripture that relate to each of The 7 Essentials and turn them into life-giving prayers for you and your peers.

Praying like the Psalmist Prays

It would be hard to have a Scripture-centered prayer guide that didn't in some way point to the primary prayer and songbook in the Bible. Therefore, we will be taking cues from the Psalms in our efforts to turn Scriptures into prayers. They reveal a plethora of ways to plead with God. There is a grittiness and authenticity in the Psalms that promotes clarity, honesty, urgency, and directness. Let's look at a few phrases from Psalm 119 that can give us a glimpse into the psalmist's directness and dependence on God in prayer:

- Do good to your servant (17)
- Open my eyes that I may see (18)
- Remove from me scorn (22)
- Preserve my life according to your word (25)
- Teach me your decrees (26)
- Let me understand the teaching of your precepts (27)
- Strengthen me (28)
- Keep me from deceitful ways (29)
- Do not let me be put to shame (31)
- Give me (34)
- Direct me (35)
- Turn my heart (36)
- Turn my eyes (37)
- Fulfill your promise (38)
- Take away (39)

- May your unfailing love (41)
- Do not snatch your word from my mouth (43)
- Remember (49)
- Be gracious (58)
- Let your compassion (77)

Each of these phrases is a clear call for God to act; a plea for the favor of God to act on the psalmists' behalf. As you turn Scripture into prayer, you are ushering a clear call for God to act on behalf of yourself and others. It is my prayer that God would be gracious to act and intervene for the good of your generation through your prayers! I pray that he would cause you to be relentless in your prayers and intentionality in making his greatness known! May God soften your heart to his greatness and grant you faithful responsiveness to his Word.

The 7 Essentials

This Prayer Guide is structured around The 7 Essentials. These seven aspects of life are the minimums that need to be attended to for you to flourish in living faithfully before God and man.

The 7 Essentials come directly from two passages of the Bible, but their importance saturates all of Scripture. The first two, wisdom and favor, come from Luke 2:52: "And Jesus increased in wisdom and in stature and in favor with God and man." When I read this verse to groups, I jokingly say, "Everyone grows in stature, except for me, so stature is not an essential." You see, I am only five foot six inches tall. I often tell my six foot six friend who played basketball for Duke that the only reason he is considered tall is because he has me to compare to. So stature, being a physical characteristic rather than spiritual, is not an essential component of flourishing in faith and life, but wisdom and favor clearly are. It is not surprising that Jesus grew in wisdom and favor because he was God in human form. What is surprising is that Luke makes sure that we know Jesus grew in wisdom and favor. Luke could have said anything he wanted about Jesus, but he made a point to let us know that growing in wisdom and favor with God and man were essential, even for the Son of God. If it was essential for God's Son to grow in wisdom and favor, then there is no question that these two are essential for us.

The other five Essentials are found in 1 Timothy 4:12: "Let no one despise you for your youth, but set the believers an example in speech, in conduct, in love, in faith, in purity." It is crucial to understand that Paul is not using throwaway words here. He is giving Timothy the essential categories that he needs to pay attention to in order to set an appropriate example for all believers. There was a lot at stake in this simple and precise directive from Paul to Timothy. These categories remain essential for us today.

The SeeSavorShare Discipleship Process

As you dive into this Prayer Guide, I want to introduce you to a simple process that can help your relationship with God flourish: SeeSavorShare (or S3 for short). S3 is about seeing the greatness of God in all of life, savoring it for all it is worth, and sharing it freely along the way. Over the last decade S3 has become the rhythm of my life with God, and I would like to encourage you to embrace it as your own as well. First, let me give you a little background concerning its value and necessity. I have been a follower of Christ since 1978 (yes I know that is a long time ago, but stay with me here). In March of 1995 God enrolled my wife and me in an intensive spiritual growth course. It was at that time that my wife began having severe migraine-like headaches. Over the next several decades, with three major surgeries and fifty-plus doctors from all across the country in our rearview mirror, her pain has not decreased but expanded to include intense muscle and bone pain that has caused countless tear-filled nights.

We have experienced the full spectrum of Western, Eastern, conventional, and unconventional medical approaches. From a Christian spiritual perspective we have experienced the full spectrum of biblical prayer and healing efforts on both individual and corporate levels. It has been in this extended season of suffering that I have had to learn to walk with God in a new way. It was during this time that I began seeking to see, savor, and share the greatness of God as a way of sustaining my relationship with him through prolonged suffering. Now I believe this is how God intended for me to live for him all along.

Anyone can live for God when the wind is at his or her back and all is well. This has not been my experience and it may not be yours. I felt like I was constantly being called on to be more than I had capacity or ability to fulfill, and S3 became, and still is, my spiritual survival process. Thankfully, you do not have to experience decades of suffering to begin seeing, savoring, and sharing the greatness of God that is all around you. You can begin the process today. S3 is the intentional process of looking for God in all of life. It is a thrilling way to walk with God and fuel a lavish love for him and others, regardless of your circumstances. It is God's desire for us to see his goodness, kindness, mercy, faithfulness, and love in all of life's situations. As he gives us a vision of his greatness in our lives, we must savor it for all it is worth with thanksgiving, praise, and adoration. It is out of the overflow of our savoring what we have seen of his greatness that we will freely share his greatness with others. This process can send life deep into your soul, just as taking in oxygen brings life to your body. S3 can become the rhythm of your life with God empowering you to flourish even in difficult times.

At the very core of S3 are three powerful truths that I encourage you to take hold of tightly and let them guide you:

1. Everything God does is great, so everything we see about who God is, what he is doing, or has done should be savored and shared.

2. We can see the greatness of God in Scripture, our daily lives, and in all of creation.

3. The Bible is the only reliable source for understanding what is true about God and what he is doing in our lives and the world around us.

Seeing

Seeing the greatness of God is the first step. The greatness of his character and works can be seen all around us. It is God's desire that we see all of the various aspects of his greatness. He wants our hearts and minds to be captured by the magnificence of his holiness, justice, righteousness, power, wisdom, goodness, patience, kindness, faithfulness, gentleness, and love. His wonders are endless! Here is something to keep in mind: if our relationship with God ever grows stale, it is not because he is not grand enough to capture the expanse of our hearts; it is because we have grown blind to the fullness of his beauty. Just as blind Bartimaeus diligently pursued Jesus to give him sight (Mark 10:46-52), so must we be intentional in asking God to give us spiritual sight to see his greatness all around us. Here are some things to remember about seeing God's greatness:

- We can see his greatness in Scripture, life, and creation.
- We can see, hear, and understand only what he enables us to, so one of our constant prayers must be for God to give us eyes to see, ears to hear, and hearts to understand his will and working in this world.

Savoring

Savoring the greatness of God that we see in Scripture, our lives, and creation is the second step of S3. Savoring is our heart's response to what we are seeing of God. It is essential to our growth with God because it is about enjoying and delighting in God and his greatness. Savoring moves us away from simply having intellectual knowledge of God and moves us closer to personally knowing him and what he cares about. Sustained savoring is absolutely crucial for our hearts to deepen in our love for God. Here are some things to remember about savoring God's greatness:

- Savoring is essential because we pursue what we love with purpose and intensity.
- Giving thanks, delighting, and treasuring are key aspects of savoring. Seek to make thankfulness your dominant mindset and heartbeat each day.
- Savoring takes time. We have to slow down and ponder what we have seen. (This will probably mean you will have to carve out time to put away all distractions like your phone, computer, tablet, etc. to focus on savoring God's goodness in your life.)
- Begin savoring by recalling times or places in your life where you have seen God's presence, protection, or provision.

Sharing

The final step in S3 is sharing. This is the natural overflow of seeing and savoring God's greatness. Sharing actually plays two primary roles for us in our growth with God. First, it completes the enjoyment of what we have seen and savored. You know the feeling when you see something incredible; you immediately begin looking around for someone to share it with. Sharing closes the circle in our enjoying the greatness of God that we have seen. Second, sharing helps us see what has a hold on our hearts. We naturally talk about what we love and enjoy. S3 is designed to help us deepen our love and enjoyment in God by seeing, savoring, and ultimately sharing his greatness with others. Here are a few things to remember about sharing God's greatness:

- Pay attention to what you talk about most. This can give you some insight into what holds the most space in your heart. The goal in this process is that you would begin to see and savor the greatness of God in your life, and sharing would naturally become the next step.
- To begin sharing, engage others about where they have seen God at work in their lives. Most people will have a time or place where they would say God has worked in their life.
- Be prepared to share stories about how you've seen God's greatness in your life. Sharing deepens your relationship with God in Christ. Philemon 6 says, "I pray that the sharing of your faith may become effective for the full knowledge of every good thing that is in us for the sake of Christ." This is a great encouragement and promise! This means every time we ask someone to share how God has worked in their lives, we are providing a means of establishing them in their faith. So don't hesitate to share, and don't hesitate to ask others to share!

S3 is included in this Prayer Guide to bring the truth about God into the present reality of your life. When you pray for your peers, remember to pray with a vision of them being captured by the greatness of God. Each day you will pray one of The 7 Essentials using S3 as your lens to help provide focus and clarity for your prayers. I pray that God would grant you favor to see and savor his

9

greatness in Scripture, life, and creation so you will be ready to share it with your generation.

Make the Prayers Your Own!

As you begin your journey through the prayers in this guide, remember to make them your own! Each prayer is written in plural form to allow you ease in praying for several people as well as yourself. There will be a tendency to read through the prayers in a rote manner; resist this tendency. Hover over the words and phrases and soak in their meaning. Find freedom in expanding and enhancing the prayers as you offer them to God.

PART TWO: A WEEK OF EACH ESSENTIAL

....

THE FAVOR FOUNDATION

One of the designs of this book is to help you make praying the Scriptures for your peers as natural as breathing. Unlike breathing, though, identifying key passages and turning them into prayers takes a little practice. As you work your way through each chapter I encourage you to start creating your own prayers. Begin identifying any words or phrases that are especially encouraging or inspiring to you as you are praying. Also, be on the hunt for portions of Scripture that you would like to make the focus of your own prayers. Remember to ask God for his favor to create prayers that will strengthen and encourage your peers.

The next seven chapters will focus on each of The 7 Essentials. There will be a short introduction to help you understand and embrace the importance of each Essential for that week. These sections will also highlight a few key Scripture passages that underscore the essence of each Essential along with some questions to ponder as you hover over the passages and prayers. Enjoy!

....

The One World Trade Center in New York City stands 1,776 feet tall, making it one of the tallest buildings in the Western Hemisphere. This is the building that was built in the very location where the World Trade Center Twin Towers fell during the 9/11 terrorist attacks. It's 408-foot spire graces the Manhattan skyline, and it's hard not to marvel at the grandeur of such a structure. But how often do we take time to consider the part of the building that makes it possible for all 104 floors to stand tall and grand? Foundations are easily forgotten and yet they are indispensible. Often times we forget that God's favor is the foundation of our lives. It is our strong and secure foundation, but in this world that values self-reliance it is easy to forget that we are completely dependent on him. Jesus is the foundation for every aspect of our lives.

He [Jesus] is the image of the invisible God, the firstborn of creation. For by Jesus all things were created, in heaven and on earth, visible and invisible, whether thrones or dominions or rulers or authorities—all things were created through Jesus and for Jesus. And Jesus is before all things, and in Jesus all things hold together. (Colossians 1:15-17)

One way to get a handle on God's favor in our lives is to realize his favor is anything he does in, through, or for you. Remember that we can see the favor of God toward us in his provision, protection, presence, and purposes. Here are several passages to help us get our heads and hearts around the immensity of God's favor:

For from him and through him and to him are all things. To him be glory forever. Amen. (Romans 11:36)

For who sees anything different in you? What do you have that you did not receive? If then you received it, why do you boast as if you did not receive it? (1 Corinthians 4:7)

Yours, O LORD, is the greatness and the power and the glory and the victory and the majesty, for all that is in the heavens and in the earth is yours. Yours is the kingdom, O LORD, and you are exalted as head above all. Both riches and honor come from you, and you rule over all. In your hand are power and might, and in your hand it is to make great and to give strength to all. And now we thank you, our God, and praise your glorious name. (1 Chronicles 29:11-13)

The God who made the world and everything in it, being Lord of heaven and earth, does not live in temples made by man, nor is he served by human hands, as though he needed anything, since he himself gives to all mankind life and breath and everything...In him we live and move and have our being. (Acts 17:24-25, 28)

I am the vine; you are the branches. Whoever abides in me and I in him, he it is that bears much fruit, for apart from me you can do nothing. (John 15:5)

Every good gift and every perfect gift is from above, coming down from the Father of lights with whom there is no variation or shadow due to change. Of his own will he brought us forth by the word of truth, that we should be a kind of firstfruits of his creatures. (James 1:17-18)

All of these passages point to God's creating and sustaining favor, upon which our entire existence rests. This is the foundation for all of the other Essentials. The importance of this Essential causes me to wonder what you and I need in order to recognize God's favor in our lives. We need eyes to see, ears to hear, and humble hearts to understand and embrace the favor of God for all it is worth. We must be diligent in praying for a posture of humility so that we might see the favor of God in his provision, protection, presence, and purposes.

One of the most important things you can do for your peers is to ask the God of the universe to show them his favor so that they might see and savor him for all that he is worth. The greatest thing in the world is to have our hearts captured by the greatness of God. So, pray diligently for yourself and your peers that God would be your greatest delight.

Pray on!

WEEK ONE // PRAYING FOR FAVOR

Give us, O Lord, a steadfast heart, which no unworthy affection may drag downwards; give us an unconquered heart, which no tribulation can wear out; give us an upright heart, which no unworthy purpose may tempt aside. Bestow upon us also, O Lord our God, understanding to know you, diligence to seek you, wisdom to find you, and a faithfulness that may finally embrace you; through Jesus Christ our Lord. —St. Thomas Aquinas

DAY ONE // FAVOR

Father, open my eyes that I might *see* you more clearly, *savor* you more fully, and *share* you more freely.

Circle or underline any key words or phrases you *See*:

But by the grace of God I am what I am, and his grace toward me was not in vain. On the contrary, I worked harder than any of them, though it was not I, but the grace of God that is with me. (1 Corinthians 15:10)

Savor these truths in prayer for yourself and others:

Father, I praise and thank you for your grace and favor. I pray that you would give _____ and me hearts that are tender and responsive to the goodness of your favor working in our lives. Awaken our minds and hearts to know and understand what the apostle Paul understood in the 1 Corinthians 15:10. That it is your ongoing grace and favor that empowers us to work diligently to glorify you and help those around us. Guard us from believing that it is by our own strength and goodness that we are making a difference in our world. Cause us to boast only in you. It is by your grace that we are who we are. You are transforming us and your work in us is never in vain. Create in us a relentless desire to be daily strengthened by your grace so that we will be tenacious in seeking to bless others for your glory and their good. In the matchless name of Jesus, amen.

Write down any thoughts you may want to *Share*:

DAY TWO // FAVOR

Father, open my eyes that I might *see* you more clearly, *savor* you more fully, and *share* you more freely.

Circle or underline any key words or phrases you *See*:

Satisfy us in the morning with your steadfast love, that we may rejoice and be glad all our days. (Psalm 90:14)

Savor these truths in prayer for yourself and others:

Father, every day _____ and I will be presented with things that promise to make us happy and satisfy the longings of our hearts. I pray that you will help us see the greatness of your steadfast love as you display it in our lives, in your Word, and in creation each day. Don't let us be tricked into believing that we would be more satisfied in life if we were smarter, stronger, prettier, or richer. You alone can satisfy our hearts and make us glad all our days. Awaken the taste buds of our hearts to enjoy the sweetness of your love every time we see it. Bring people into our lives that will help us delight in loving you. Help us learn to share our joy in your love more naturally and freely with others each day. For your glory and our good, in the all-satisfying name of Jesus, amen.

Write down any thoughts you may want to *Share*:

DAY THREE // FAVOR

Father, open my eyes that I might *see* you more clearly, *savor* you more fully, and *share* you more freely.

Circle or underline any key words or phrases you *See:*

"Glory to God in the highest, and on earth peace among those with whom he is pleased!" (Luke 2:14)
Now may the Lord of peace himself give you peace at all times in every way. The Lord be with you all. (2 Thessalonians 3:16)

Savor these truths in prayer for yourself and others:

Father, when your angels announced Jesus' arrival in the world, they declared glory to you and peace to us. Thank you that Jesus' coming declares your glory and our need. I pray for _____ and myself, that you would create in us a longing for the peace that you offer to the world through Jesus. Help us to identify any fears or anxieties that reside in our hearts about anything and bring them to you, that you would reign over them with your peace that surpasses all understanding. Help us to know that your peace in Jesus brings freedom that the world does not know. Cause us to become peacemakers to those around us. For your glory and our good, in the name of the Prince of Peace, Jesus, amen.

Write down any thoughts you may want to *Share:*

DAY FOUR // FAVOR

Father, open my eyes that I might *see* you more clearly, *savor* you more fully, and *share* you more freely.

Circle or underline any key words or phrases you *See*:

What then shall we say to these things? If God is for us, who can be against us? He who did not spare his own Son but gave him up for us all, how will he not also with him graciously give us all things? (Romans 8:31-32)

Savor these truths in prayer for yourself and others:

Father, I pray today that _____ and I would sense the magnitude of your favor and goodness toward us. Let us be amazed by the fact that you are more than enough for whatever we face in this life. Let the truth that you are "for" us give us unbelievable courage to live for you in spite of our fears. Cause our confidence in you to be matched by a growing dependence on you, seeking your presence, protection, and provision each day. Show us that all the resources of heaven are ours in Jesus. You have given the greatest gift of all in Jesus and I pray you would let the significance of his life, death, and resurrection sink into the depths of our hearts. Cause our trust in you to increase because of the truths of Romans 8:31-32. For your glory and our good, in Jesus' name, amen.

Write down any thoughts you may want to *Share*:

DAY FIVE // FAVOR

Father, open my eyes that I might *see* you more clearly, *savor* you more fully, and *share* you more freely.

Circle or underline any key words or phrases you *See*:

Let the favor of the Lord our God be upon us, and establish the work of our hands upon us; yes, establish the work of our hands! (Psalm 90:17)

Savor these truths in prayer for yourself and others:

Father, I pray that _____ and I would know your favor in our work today, whether at school or our jobs or at home. Help us to realize that whatever we set our hands to do should be for your glory. You have created us for good works and we should devote ourselves fully to the work to which you have called us. Establish the work of our hands, giving us a sense of accomplishment. Make it clear that your hand of favor is upon us through your provision, protection, presence, and purposes. Encourage us to find joy in our work, and make us a joy to work with. Cause us to study with diligence and delight in the truths we learn. For your glory and our good, in Jesus' name, amen.

Write down any thoughts you may want to *Share*:

DAY SIX // FAVOR

Father, open my eyes that I might *see* you more clearly, *savor* you more fully, and *share* you more freely.

Circle or underline any key words or phrases you *See*:

It is he who remembered us in our low estate, for his steadfast love endures forever; and rescued us from our foes, for his steadfast love endures forever; he who gives food to all flesh, for his steadfast love endures forever. Give thanks to the God of heaven, for his steadfast love endures forever. (Psalm 136:23-26)

Savor these truths in prayer for yourself and others:

Father, your steadfast love for _____ and me endures forever. It is through your grace and favor that we are able to know and experience your steadfast love toward us. If we are discouraged today, give us hope by reminding us that you love us. I pray that you would guard, protect, and rescue us from harm, and help us to have discernment in judging the intentions of others. Give us eyes to see the goodness of your provision every time we sit down to a meal. Stir up enduring thankfulness in us toward you and your favor. For your glory and our good, in the matchless name of Jesus, amen.

Write down any thoughts you may want to *Share*:

21

DAY SEVEN // FAVOR

Father, open my eyes that I might *see* you more clearly, *savor* you more fully, and *share* you more freely.

Circle or underline any key words or phrases you *See*:

He [Jesus] is the image of the invisible God, the firstborn of all creation. For by him all things were created, in heaven and on earth, visible and invisible, whether thrones or dominions or rulers or authorities—all things were created through him and for him. And he is before all things, and in him all things hold together. (Colossians 1:15-17)

Savor these truths in prayer for yourself and others:

Father, thank you that you create and sustain all things. Your Word declares that every day we are receiving your matchless favor through the sustaining power and goodness of Jesus. I pray that _____ and I would have a clear sense that we were not only created by Jesus, but also for Jesus. Fill our hearts and minds with delight in you that overflows in what we say and do. Let our lives give others hope in you as the creator and sustainer of life. Cause our delight in Jesus to continually increase, so that each day we would seek a deeper understanding of all that He is. For your glory and our good, in the matchless name of King Jesus, amen.

Write down any thoughts you may want to *Share*:

NOTES

THE CORE FOUR

....

WISDOM

The next four chapters will focus on what I call the Core Four of the Essentials: wisdom, love, faith, and purity. They reflect the core elements needed to flourish in our relationship with God and others, and they are the ingredients that represent the core substance of who we are. God desires for us to be marked by these core four, and it is in these areas that we need God to unleash his favor first and foremost.

....

Who is the wisest person you know? What about them makes them wise? When I ask about the wisest person you know, I'm not necessarily talking about who is the smartest. Wisdom goes farther than just being smart. It incorporates other qualities like goodness, mercy, and justice, but it doesn't stop there. Wisdom is the ability to understand what motivates people.

When I think about the wisest people of all time, there are two names that rise to the top of my list. Both are found in the Bible. One is King Solomon from the Old Testament who God made to be the wisest king to ever live. The other is Jesus, the Son of God, who was fully God and fully man and whom the Bible points to as the wisest person of all time. In fact, Colossians 2:3 says, "In [Jesus] are hidden all the treasures of wisdom and knowledge."

Wisdom Spotlight

There is a great example of Solomon's wisdom in action in the third chapter of 1 Kings. I already mentioned that God made him the wisest king to ever live. Let's look at how that came to pass. The context of this story takes place after King David dies. This is the same David that faced Goliath and gave him a permanent headache by landing a precision strike in his forehead with a stone launched from his slingshot. (That is a great story that you can read for yourself in detail in 1 Samuel 17.) David went on to become a great king over the nation of Israel. David had a son named Solomon who became King over all of Israel when David died. As you can imagine, this was a lot of responsibility and pressure for a young man. Early in Solomon's reign as king, God appeared to him in a dream and asked Solomon what he would like him to do for him. This was a blank check offer from the God of the universe—Solomon could have asked for whatever he wanted and received it! Knowing this, Solomon asked for a discerning mind to know the difference between good and evil.

In the end, Solomon received wisdom and so much more. Because God was so pleased that Solomon didn't ask out of personal selfishness, he went ahead and gave Solomon riches and greatness along with the promise of a long life so long as he kept God's commands. He needed wisdom so he asked for it and went on to become the wisest man to ever live apart from Jesus.

Now let's look at the story that put Solomon's wisdom to the test. There were two women who each had newborn infants. One of the babies died during the night when his mother accidentally laid on him. Upon waking and finding her baby dead, she proceeded to switch her baby for the other woman's child while she slept. When the second mother awoke to find the dead infant next to her she was heart broken. She then began looking closely

at the child only to realize it wasn't hers. They brought their di-
lemma to the king, each woman claiming the living child as her
own. Solomon put his wisdom into action and called for a sword
to be brought so that he could cut the child in half and give each
mother a share. With this news, the true mother of the child pro-
tested and said that the other woman should have the child so that
he may live. The mother of the dead child liked the idea and said,
"he shall neither be mine nor yours; divide him." This was the
clincher. Solomon knew that the true mother would do whatever
was necessary to let her son live. 1 Kings 3:27 says "Then the king
answered and said, 'Give the living child to the first woman, and by
no means put him to death; she is his mother.'" I love how the
chapter finishes: "All of Israel heard about the judgment the king
had rendered, and they stood in awe of the him, because they perceived that the wisdom of God was in him to do justice" (1 Kings
3:28).

Having wisdom is absolutely crucial if we want to flourish
in this life. Being wise affects everything we say, think, and do.
Every aspect of our lives is touched by our wisdom or the lack
thereof. The Bible has a lot to say about wisdom and what it means
to become a wise young man or woman. Consider the book of Proverbs, which is written by our friend Solomon. It is an entire book,
right in the middle of the Bible, that focuses on wisdom and is
specifically written to provide knowledge and discretion to young
people (Proverbs 1:4). If you were to read through the book of Proverbs you would find that it is ultimately impossible to get the most
out of this life without embracing the pursuit of wisdom. Becoming
wise does not just happen by accident or in a casual way though.
We cannot coast into becoming a wise person; we have to seriously
and intentionally pursue it.

Pursuing Jesus for Deep Wisdom

One of my favorite passages about gaining wisdom or becoming wise is Colossians 2:3, where the apostle Paul says that "in [Jesus] are hidden all the treasures of wisdom and knowledge." If you really want to be wise you will have to get up close and personal with Jesus. Or put another way, to be truly wise you must bring what you think, say, and do into alignment with who Jesus is and what his purposes are in the world. You must learn to see the world through the lens of the person and work of Jesus.

With this in mind one of the questions I'm learning to frequently ask myself and others is this: how well do you really know the person and purposes of Jesus? What is it about Jesus that makes him so compelling? The Bible tells us that not only is Jesus massively compelling, but he is also the source of wisdom. We must learn to mine the treasures of wisdom and knowledge that are hidden in Christ.

Here is a key point: If we are not seeing the wondrous treasures that are hidden in Christ we will not pray as fervently as we should for our peers to taste and see the depths of wisdom that are held in Jesus. One of our first prayers should be for God to open our eyes so that we might see and savor the sweetness of the wisdom and knowledge that is in Jesus. Then we can share freely whether through prayer or in person with our peers. May our hearts be deeply satisfied in Jesus and all of his greatness.

Practically Speaking

Andy Stanley is a pastor and author who has written numerous books, one of which was called *The Best Question Ever* when it was first published. Now it is called simply *Ask It*. The best question ever, according to Andy, is "What is the wise thing to do?" Andy identifies this question as being at the heart of what the apostle Paul was commanding in Ephesians 5:15-17: "Look carefully then how you walk, not as unwise but as wise, making the best use of the time, because the days are evil. Therefore do not be foolish, but understand what the will of the Lord is."

This is such a simple question but it is by far one of the most *regret reducing* questions you can ever ask yourself. Even if you don't do the absolute wisest thing, you will be saving yourself massive heartache when you make decisions that lean strongly in the direction of wisdom. This is true for your friends too. So, as you become a Prayer Champion for your generation, praying for growth in wisdom is one of the best things you can do.

Pray on!

WEEK TWO // PRAYING FOR WISDOM

Besides being wise, the Preacher also taught the people knowledge, weighing and studying and arranging many proverbs with great care. The Preacher sought to find words of delight, and uprightly he wrote words of truth. The words of the wise are like goads, and like nails firmly fixed are the collected sayings; they are given by one Shepherd. My son, beware of anything beyond these. Of making many books there is no end, and much study is a weariness of the flesh. The end of the matter; all has been heard. Fear God and keep his commandments, for this is the whole duty of man. For God will bring every deed into judgment, with every secret thing, whether good or evil. (Ecclesiastes 12:9-14)

DAY ONE // WISDOM

Father, open my eyes that I might *see* you more clearly, *savor* you more fully, and *share* you more freely.

Circle or underline any key words or phrases you *See*:

Thus says the LORD: "Let not the wise man boast in his wisdom, let not the mighty man boast in his might, let not the rich man boast in his riches, but let him who boasts boast in this, that he understands and knows me, that I am the LORD who practices steadfast love, justice, and righteousness in the earth. For in these things I delight, declares the LORD." (Jeremiah 9:23-24)

Savor these truths in prayer for yourself and others:

Father, I pray today that _____ and I would not boast or try to find our identity in how smart or insightful we are. Protect us from the lure of believing that our intelligence or insight makes us superior (or inferior) to other people. Cause our identity to be deeply rooted in you and our relationship with you, knowing that all of our abilities are gifts from you. Give us the wisdom that only comes from you to see where your love, justice, and righteousness are needed. Don't let us become cold or indifferent to the hardships around us. Give us a relentless resolve to apply your wisdom to these situations whole-heartedly, even when it is hard. Help us to encourage others and affirm all of the wisdom we see flowing from their lives. For your glory and our good, in Jesus' name, amen.

Write down any thoughts you may want to *Share*:

DAY TWO // WISDOM

Father, open my eyes that I might *see* you more clearly, *savor* you more fully, and *share* you more freely.

Circle or underline any key words or phrases you *See*:

Let no one deceive himself. If anyone among you thinks that he is wise in this age, let him become a fool that he may become wise. For the wisdom of this world is folly with God. For it is written, "He catches the wise in their craftiness," and again, "The Lord knows the thoughts of the wise, that they are futile." So let no one boast in men. For all things are yours, whether Paul or Apollos or Cephas or the world or life or death or the present or the future—all are yours, and you are Christ's, and Christ is God's. (1 Corinthians 3:18-23)

Savor these truths in prayer for yourself and others:

Father, it is so easy to be deceived into thinking that the ways of this world are wise. It is also easy to deceive ourselves into thinking we are wise on our own. I pray that you would protect _____ and me from traveling the path of self-proclaimed wisdom, which is really the way of foolishness. Give us a keen sense of dependence on you so we can walk in humble confidence in you. Help us see the futility of trying to live by wisdom that is not rooted in you. Give us joy in turning to you in complete reliance, knowing that all things are yours and therefore our boast should be in you. Give us pleasure in you as the source of all truth. Lastly, help us also to love and long for your wisdom above our own. For your glory and our good, in the supreme name of Christ, amen.

Write down any thoughts you may want to *Share*:

DAY THREE // WISDOM

Father, open my eyes that I might *see* you more clearly, *savor* you more fully, and *share* you more freely.

Circle or underline any key words or phrases you *See*:

I do not cease to give thanks for you, remembering you in my prayers, that the God of our Lord Jesus Christ, the Father of glory, may give you the Spirit of wisdom and of revelation in the knowledge of him, having the eyes of your hearts enlightened, that you may know what is the hope to which he has called you, what are the riches of his glorious inheritance in the saints, and what is the immeasurable greatness of his power toward us who believe, according to the working of his great might that he worked in Christ when he raised him from the dead... (Ephesians 1:16-20)

Savor these truths in prayer for yourself and others:

Father, I pray that you would give _____ and me your Spirit of wisdom, revelation, and knowledge. Enlighten the eyes of our hearts so that we might be eager to receive all the goodness that comes from each of these gifts. Cause us to have an unwavering hope in the glorious inheritance you have prepared for us. Help us to find rest and strength in your immeasurable power—the same power that raised Jesus from the dead. Empower us to live lives fueled by your Spirit. Make us like the apostle Paul who was a man of relentless thankfulness and purposeful prayer. For your glory and our good, in Jesus' name, amen.

Write down any thoughts you may want to *Share*:

DAY FOUR // WISDOM

Father, open my eyes that I might *see* you more clearly, *savor* you more fully, and *share* you more freely.

Circle or underline any key words or phrases you *See*:

Walk in wisdom toward outsiders, making the best use of the time. (Colossians 4:5)

Look carefully then how you walk, not as unwise but as wise, making the best use of the time, because the days are evil. Therefore do not be foolish, but understand what the will of the Lord is. And do not get drunk with wine, for that is debauchery, but be filled with the Spirit... (Ephesians 5:15-18)

Savor these truths in prayer for yourself and others:

Father, I pray today for _____ and myself, that we would walk in wisdom in all of our relationships. Cause us to understand that our choices matter and to know that every decision leads to a destination. Give us incredible delight and persistence in turning away from evil and making the best use of our time. Give us a powerful desire to pursue your purposes with the time you have given us. Give us confidence that your will can be found in your Word. Your Word is the sword of the Spirit that is able to cut through the lies of this world. Give us a relentless desire to drink deeply of your Word every day so that we will be filled with your Spirit. For your glory and our good, in Jesus' name, amen.

Write down any thoughts you may want to *Share*:

33

DAY FIVE // WISDOM

Father, open my eyes that I might *see* you more clearly, *savor* you more fully, and *share* you more freely.

Circle or underline any key words or phrases you *See*:

For I want you to know how great a struggle I have for you and for those at Laodicea and for all who have not seen me face to face, that their hearts may be encouraged, being knit together in love, to reach all the riches of full assurance of understanding and the knowledge of God's mystery, which is Christ, in whom are hidden all the treasures of wisdom and knowledge. I say this in order that no one may delude you with plausible arguments. (Colossians 2:1-4)

Savor these truths in prayer for yourself and others:

Father, please give _____ and me hearts that are full of encouragement because they are unshakably bound in your love. Cause us to reach the fullness of knowing and understanding your mystery, which is Christ. Give us a deep understanding and joy in all the treasures of wisdom and knowledge that are hidden in Christ. May we flourish in seeing, savoring, and sharing the depths of wisdom and knowledge of Jesus with our friends. Let us be so captivated by the wonder of Jesus that we would never be duped to hope in something or someone else for life and joy. For your glory and our good, in Jesus' name, amen.

Write down any thoughts you may want to *Share*:

DAY SIX // WISDOM

Father, open my eyes that I might *see* you more clearly, *savor* you more fully, and *share* you more freely.

Circle or underline any key words or phrases you *See*:

But as for you, continue in what you have learned and have firmly believed, knowing from whom you learned it and how from childhood you have been acquainted with the sacred writings, which are able to make you wise for salvation through faith in Christ Jesus. All Scripture is breathed out by God and profitable for teaching, for reproof, for correction, and for training in righteousness, that the man of God may be complete, equipped for every good work. (2 Timothy 3:14-17)

Savor these truths in prayer for yourself and others:

Father, there is nothing more important than knowing you personally. Create in _____ and me tender hearts that are responsive to your Word so that we become wise for salvation through faith in Christ Jesus. Don't let us be deceived by the lies of this world; assure us that Jesus is the only way by which we can be saved and made right with you. Create in us teachable hearts and minds so that we may receive the full benefits of engaging with your Word. Bring people into our lives that help us grow to love your Word. Cause us to flourish in living out the truths of your Word. For your glory and our good, in Jesus' name, amen.

Write down any thoughts you may want to *Share*:

DAY SEVEN // WISDOM

Father, open my eyes that I might *see* you more clearly, *savor* you more fully, and *share* you more freely.

Circle or underline any key words or phrases you *See*:

Who is wise and understanding among you? By his good conduct let him show his works in the meekness of wisdom…But the wisdom from above is first pure, then peaceable, gentle, open to reason, full of mercy and good fruits, impartial and sincere. And a harvest of righteousness is sown in peace by those who make peace. (James 3:13, 17-18)

Savor these truths in prayer for yourself and others:

Father, wise people bear fruit that reveals your wisdom. I pray that you would give _____ and me a hunger and thirst for your wisdom that is clearly a gift from you. Cause us to pursue it with diligent humility, leaving behind us a host of lives blessed by the fruit of the wisdom from above. Give us a keen ability to spot wisdom that is from you and embrace it as our own. Cause us to bear the fruit of wisdom that is pure, peaceful, gentle, open to reason, impartial, and sincere. Bring people into our lives who know and live out your wise purposes. May our lives produce a harvest of righteousness that is sown in peace. For your glory and our good, in the precious name of Jesus, amen.

Write down any thoughts you may want to *Share*:

NOTES

PRAYER THOUGHTS

Prayer is the definitive act of displaying our dependence on God, showing His all-sufficient Greatness and our all-encompassing need for Him.

"Call to me and I will answer you, and will tell you great and hidden things that you have not known." Jeremiah 33:3

"Call upon me in the day of trouble; I will deliver you, and you shall glorify me." Psalm 50:15

God works on behalf of those who wait for Him! Prayer is the primary way of waiting on God. Continue to pursue God for yourself and others in prayer.

"From of old no one has heard or perceived by the ear, no eye has seen a God besides you, who acts for those who wait for him." Isaiah 64:4

Colossians 4:12 gives us a great example of what it looks like to be tenacious on behalf of others in prayer.

"Epaphras, who is one of you, a servant of Christ Jesus, greets you, always struggling on your behalf in his prayers, that you may stand mature and fully assured in all the will of God." Colossians 4:12

THE CORE FOUR

....

LOVE

Praying for love for your generation means coming to terms with the centrality of love in God's character. Take a look at the following verses:

Anyone who does not love does not know God, because God is love. (1 John 4:8)

So we have come to know and to believe the love that God has for us. God is love, and whoever abides in love abides in God, and God abides in him. (1 John 4:16)

So now faith, hope, and love abide, these three; but the greatest of these is love. (1 Corinthians 13:13)

And he said to him, "You shall love the Lord your God with all your heart and with all your soul and with all your mind. This is the great and first commandment. And a second is like it: You shall love your neighbor as yourself. On these two commandments depend all the Law and the Prophets. (Matthew 22:37-40)

It may be easy to breeze right by these passages because you've heard them before, but slow down and let these truths sink in. Think about the power of what Jesus is saying in Matthew 22. Everything that God has said in the Law and the Prophets (which

39

is basically the Old Testament) can be summed up in two divine directives: love God supremely and love others the way we love ourselves. Wow! This is why love is one of the Core Four.

God Really Does Love Us!

It would be hard to overstate how important it is for us to comprehend how much God loves us. That is why I believe the apostle Paul was so intentionally focused on knowing the love of God when he prayed for the believers in Ephesus:

For this reason I bow my knees before the Father, from whom every family in heaven and on earth is named, that according to the riches of his glory he may grant you to be strengthened with power through his Spirit in your inner being, so that Christ may dwell in your hearts through faith— that you, being rooted and grounded in love, may have strength to comprehend with all the saints what is the breadth and length and height and depth, and to know the love of Christ that surpasses knowledge, that you may be filled with all the fullness of God. (Ephesians 3:14-19)

Did you see the second to last part of that prayer? Paul is praying that the believers would know the love of Christ that surpasses knowledge! The magnitude of the love of Christ surpasses normal knowledge and yet Paul prays that they would actually know the unknowable. I pray this for you as well! I pray that you will find great joy in praying something this big for yourself and your peers.

Love Spotlight

There are many stories and passages in the Bible that show us what true love is, but none is more specifically focused than 1 Corinthians 13. It describes how love functions in the practical aspects of life.

If I speak in the tongues of men and of angels, but have not love, I am a noisy gong or a clanging cymbal. And if I have prophetic powers, and understand all mysteries and all knowledge, and if I have all faith, so as to remove mountains, but have not love, I am nothing. If I give away all I have, and if I deliver up my body to be burned, but have not love, I gain nothing.

Love is patient and kind; love does not envy or boast; it is not arrogant or rude. It does not insist on its own way; it is not irritable or resentful; it does not rejoice at wrongdoing, but rejoices with the truth. Love bears all things, believes all things, hopes all things, endures all things.

Love never ends. As for prophecies, they will pass away; as for tongues, they will cease; as for knowledge, it will pass away. For we know in part and we prophesy in part, but when the perfect comes, the partial will pass away. When I was a child, I spoke like a child, I thought like a child, I reasoned like a child. When I became a man, I gave up childish ways. For now we see in a mirror dimly, but then face to face. Now I know in part; then I shall know fully, even as I have been fully known. So now faith, hope, and love abide, these three; but the greatest of these is love. (1 Corinthians 13:1-14:1)

As you read this you may think it's impossible for you to ever live up to this kind of love, and you're right if you are trying to do it on your own. But remember this: *Jesus' life fulfills this chapter perfectly.* You might be tempted to say, "that's because he is God," and that's what I said for many years. But Jesus' life shows us what can happen when someone is fully yielded to the Holy Spirit. Jesus loved well because he depended on the Holy Spirit and we are called to walk as Jesus walked. It is as we yield to the power of the Holy Spirit that we are able to love those in our world well, making it clear that we are followers of Christ. Consider John 13:34 and 35:

"A new commandment I give you, that you love one another: just as I have loved you, you also are to love one another. By this all people will know that you are my disciples, if you have love for one another." God the Holy Spirit comes to live inside of you when you become a follower of Jesus. His role is to empower you to be conformed into the image of Jesus over time as you yield and submit to his leadership in your life. Ask God to grant you his favor to love the way he has called you to love.

Pursue love. Pray on!

WEEK THREE // PRAYING FOR LOVE

To be grateful is to recognize the Love of God in everything He has given us—and He has given us everything. Every breath we draw is a gift of His Love, every moment of existence is a grace, for it brings with it immense graces from Him. — Don Postema

And whatever you do, in word or deed, do everything in the name of the Lord Jesus, giving thanks to God the Father through him. (Colossians 3:17)

...pray without ceasing, give thanks in all circumstances; for this is the will of God in Christ Jesus for you. (1 **Thessalonians** 5:17-18)

DAY ONE // LOVE

Father, open my eyes that I might *see* you more clearly, *savor* you more fully, and *share* you more freely.

Circle or underline any key words or phrases you *See*:

Love is patient and kind; love does not envy or boast; it is not arrogant or rude. It does not insist on its own way; it is not irritable or resentful; it does not rejoice at wrongdoing, but rejoices with the truth. Love bears all things, believes all things, hopes all things, endures all things. Love never ends. As for prophecies, they will pass away; as for tongues, they will cease; as for knowledge, it will pass away. (1 Corinthians 13:4-8)

Savor these truths in prayer for yourself and others:

Father, your love endures forever! I pray today that _____ and I would receive your love through other people. Grant that we would know your patience and feel your kindness throughout this day. Give us favor to encounter people filled with your love today. Cause us to become people who are marked by your love, showing patience and kindness especially when we encounter people who are arrogant and rude. May we be the sweet aroma of Christ to people who insist on their own way. Cause your supernatural love to empower us to believe, hope, and endure all things. For your glory and our good, in Jesus' name, amen.

Write down any thoughts you may want to *Share*:

DAY TWO // LOVE

Father, open my eyes that I might *see* you more clearly, *savor* you more fully, and *share* you more freely.

Circle or underline any key words or phrases you *See*:

A new commandment I give to you, that you love one another: just as I have loved you, you also are to love one another. By this all people will know that you are my disciples, if you have love for one another. (John 13:34-35)

Savor these truths in prayer for yourself and others:

Father, I pray for _____ and myself today, that we would embrace your commandment to love one another. Give us eyes to see and hearts to understand how you have personally loved us. In your goodness provide us insight into just how deep, wide, long, and high your love is for us. Create in us a strong desire and will to show love to others. May our obedience to your command to love one another cause the people in our lives to know that we are your disciples. Protect us from becoming casual or indifferent in how we care for those around us. Help us experience your love deeply so we can love others deeply. Show us how we can be agents of your love. For your glory and our good, in Jesus' name, amen.

Write down any thoughts you may want to *Share*:

DAY THREE // LOVE

Father, open my eyes that I might *see* you more clearly, *savor* you more fully, and *share* you more freely.

Circle or underline any key words or phrases you *See*:

There is no fear in love, but perfect love casts out fear. For fear has to do with punishment, and whoever fears has not been perfected in love. We love because he first loved us. If anyone says, "I love God," and hates his brother, he is a liar; for he who does not love his brother whom he has seen cannot love God whom he has not seen. And this commandment we have for him: whoever loves God must also love his brother. (1 John 4:18-21)

Savor these truths in prayer for yourself and others:

Father, give _____ and me eyes to see our fears and help us to have complete confidence that your perfect love can neutralize those fears. Cause us to run to you with each and every fear so that they may be swallowed up by your perfect love. There is a profound freedom that comes from knowing your deep and abiding love. Help our hearts soak in your fear-killing and freedom-producing love like a brand new sponge. Where our love is weak, strengthen it. Make our hearts grow large in love towards you and others. Help us to learn to love others in the same way they have received love from you. For your glory and our good, in the loving name of Jesus, amen.

Write down any thoughts you may want to *Share*:

DAY FOUR // LOVE

Father, open my eyes that I might *see* you more clearly, *savor* you more fully, and *share* you more freely.

Circle or underline any key words or phrases you *See*:

In this the love of God was made manifest among us, that God sent his only Son into the world, so that we might live through him. In this is love, not that we have loved God but that he loved us and sent his Son to be the propitiation for our sins. Beloved, if God so loved us, we also ought to love one another. (1 John 4:9-11)

Savor these truths in prayer for yourself and others:

Father, thank you for making your love clear in Jesus! I pray that you would give _____ and me an ever-deepening sense of the importance of your love for us in sending your Son into the world. Help us see that our sins have separated us from you, and you solved that separation through Jesus' sacrifice. Let us understand your amazing goodness in sending Jesus to take the full amount of your wrath for our sins. Cause our hearts to be filled with overflowing thankfulness for your sacrificial love. May that love be one of the distinguishing marks of our lives. Help us love one another the way that you have loved us in Jesus. Give us eyes to see how we can show your love to others today. For your glory and our good, in Jesus' name, amen.

Write down any thoughts you may want to *Share*:

DAY FIVE // LOVE

Father, open my eyes that I might *see* you more clearly, *savor* you more fully, and *share* you more freely.

Circle or underline any key words or phrases you *See*:

For God so loved the world, that he gave his only Son, that who-ever believes in him should not perish but have eternal life. For God did not send his Son into the world to condemn the world, but in order that the world might be saved through him. Whoever believes in him is not condemned, but whoever does not believe is condemned already, because he has not believed in the name of the only Son of God. (John 3:16-18)

Savor these truths in prayer for yourself and others:

Father, I pray that in your grace you would be generous in giving _____ and me eyes to see the scope of your love for the world. The world is big and yet your love is even bigger. Create in us a desire to grow in our understanding of the depth of your personal sacrifice by sending your Son, Jesus to pay the penalty for our sins. Increase our confidence that Jesus is the only way of entering eternal life. Help us learn to embrace the weight of the truth that not believing in Jesus, the only Son of God, results in condemnation. Give us a relentless desire to invite unbelievers to put their trust in Jesus alone for life, a life that starts now and lasts forever. For your glory and our good, in the saving name of Jesus, amen.

Write down any thoughts you may want to *Share*:

DAY SIX // LOVE

Father, open my eyes that I might *see* you more clearly, *savor* you more fully, and *share* you more freely.

Circle or underline any key words or phrases you *See*:

Beloved, let us love one another, for love is from God, and whoever loves has been born of God and knows God. Anyone who does not love does not know God, because God is love. (1 John 4:7-8)

Savor these truths in prayer for yourself and others:

Father, I pray for _____ and myself, that you would open our eyes to see that you are the source of all love, because you are love. I pray that you would be lavish in pouring your love into our lives. Grant that we would grow in our understanding of what it means to know you and to be born of you. Cause us to love others deeply out of our own growing relationship with you. Keep us from ever minimizing the importance of loving others well. Help us to be aware of any tendency to shrug it off or take it lightly when we hold onto a grudge, are bitter, or disrespectful of others. Help us to embrace the truth that without a life marked by love, we cannot really know you because you are love! For your glory and our good, in Jesus' name, amen.

Write down any thoughts you may want to *Share*:

DAY SEVEN // LOVE

Father, open my eyes that I might *see* you more clearly, *savor* you more fully, and *share* you more freely.

Circle or underline any key words or phrases you *See*:

"But I say to you who hear, Love your enemies, do good to those who hate you, bless those who curse you, pray for those who abuse you... "If you love those who love you, what benefit is that to you? For even sinners love those who love them... Be merciful, even as your Father is merciful. (Luke 6:27-28, 33, 36)

Savor these truths in prayer for yourself and others:

Father, thank you that your love is unlike anything the world has ever known. I pray that _____ and I would taste and see that you are good and that your love has power to transform relationships. Help us to embrace your desire for us to love our enemies by doing them good and praying for them. Help us to see when our response to our enemies looks more like the world's than yours. In your mercy, I pray that you would give us hearts that are filled with mercy toward others. Cause us to see that how we treat others, especially our adversaries, is really important. May you receive great glory from our obedience in loving the most difficult to love. For your glory and our good, in the all-powerful name of Jesus Christ, amen.

Write down any thoughts you may want to *Share*:

NOTES

THE CORE FOUR

....

FAITH

There are numerous passages in the Bible about the importance of faith in our relationship with God. One of my favorites is Hebrews 11:6: "Without faith it is impossible to please him, for whoever would draw near to God must believe that he exists and that he rewards those who seek him." There is so much sustaining goodness about faith and God and us wrapped up in this one little verse. When a person has faith in God it naturally moves them toward him. Faith believes there is a God, that he exists, and that he is not aloof, but he actually cares for us and wants to bless those who seek him.

There is an important point hidden in the very fabric of this passage on faith: prayer and faith go together. You can pray and not have faith, but you cannot have faith and not pray. To have faith in him means you will have to learn to pray well. Those who believe they are walking with God well and are not praying are like a person who is trying to live without breathing. It certainly can be done, but not for very long.

Another aspect of this passage is that our heavenly Father wants to reward or bless us when we seek him in prayer. We may not receive the very thing we are asking for, but almost invariably we will get more of his presence in our lives. Getting more of God is always the best gift no matter what we may have been seeking originally.

Faith Spotlight

There is a plethora (I love that word) or an overabundance of stories in the Bible that we could use as our faith spotlight, but let's look at a slice of the life of Nehemiah from the book that bears his name. It comes from the first chapter and powerfully illustrates how we can trust and seek God when we face difficulties. Nehemiah serves as the cupbearer to Artaxerxes, King of Persia, which means he was a person of irreproachable loyalty and trustworthiness. It was his responsibility to make sure no one was trying to poison the king. While he was cupbearer he received word that his people were living in shame and danger because the walls of the city of Jerusalem had been torn down. The following story is Nehemiah's immediate response. As you read through, take note of how Nehemiah engages with God in prayer. What does he reveal about his knowledge of God, himself, and how he seeks to trust God in the face of his challenge?

As soon as I heard these words I sat down and wept and mourned for days, and I continued fasting and praying before the God of heaven. And I said, "O LORD God of heaven, the great and awesome God who keeps covenant and steadfast love with those who love him and keep his commandments, let your ear be attentive and your eyes open, to hear the prayer of your servant that I now pray before you day and night for the people of Israel your servants, confessing the sins of the people of Israel, which we have sinned against you. Even I and my father's house have sinned. We have acted very corruptly against you and have not kept the commandments, the statutes, and the rules that you commanded your servant Moses. Remember the word that you commanded your servant

Moses, saying, 'If you are unfaithful, I will scatter you among the peoples, but if you return to me and keep my commandments and do them, though your outcasts are in the uttermost parts of heaven, from there I will gather them and bring them to the place that I have chosen, to make my name dwell there.' They are your servants and your people, whom you have re-deemed by your great power and by your strong hand. O Lord, let your ear be attentive to the prayer of your servant, and to the prayer of your servants who delight to fear your name, and give success to your servant today, and grant him mercy in the sight of this man." (Nehemiah 1:4-11)

Nehemiah sets an example for us here by responding with total faith and dependence on God in the midst of difficulty. Here are three takeaways from the passage:

1. *Nehemiah cared deeply about injustice,* which com-pelled him to weep, pray, and act in faith. Keep a pulse on what you care deeply about that moves you to pray and step out in faith.
2. *Nehemiah yielded himself to the greatness of God* in prayer by confessing and repenting of sin on behalf of himself and the people of Israel. Make a habit of yielding your life to God's greatness through daily confession and repentance.
3. *Nehemiah knew and believed the promises of God* and relied on his provision as he stepped out in faith to advance the purposes of God. What are some of the promises of God that are empowering you to trust him?

As you pray for yourself and those around you, remember to appeal to the power, promises, and character of God. Pray on!

WEEK FOUR // PRAYING FOR FAITH

You can pray and not have faith, but you cannot have faith and not pray. To have faith in him means you will have to learn to pray well. Those who believe they are walking with God well and are not praying are like a person who is trying to live without breathing. It certainly can be done, but not for very long.

DAY ONE // FAITH

Father, open my eyes that I might *see* you more clearly, *savor* you more fully, and *share* you more freely.

Circle or underline any key words or phrases you *See*:

And without faith it is impossible to please him, for whoever would draw near to God must believe that he exists and that he rewards those who seek him. (Hebrews 11:6)

Savor these truths in prayer for yourself and others:

Father, I pray for _____ and myself today, that you would capture our hearts and minds with the truths of this passage. Instill in our hearts a relentless desire to please you. Protect us from the cultural disease of indifference or apathy concerning what pleases you. Help us to understand that without faith it is impossible to please you. Teach us to take you at your Word and turn to Scripture with every struggle we encounter. Give us faith to believe that you are alive and ready to work on our behalf when we seek you with our whole hearts. Be the object of our faith, and may our reward be a heart that is satisfied with all that you are for us. For your glory and our good, in Jesus' name, amen.

Write down any thoughts you may want to *Share*:

DAY TWO // FAITH

Father, open my eyes that I might *see* you more clearly, *savor* you more fully, and *share* you more freely.

Circle or underline any key words or phrases you *See*:

Therefore, since we are surrounded by so great a cloud of witnesses, let us also lay aside every weight, and sin which clings so closely, and let us run with endurance the race that is set before us, looking to Jesus, the founder and perfecter of our faith, who for the joy that was set before him endured the cross, despising the shame, and is seated at the right hand of the throne of God. (Hebrews 12:1-2)

Savor these truths in prayer for yourself and others:

Father, thank you for calling _____ and me to run the race of faith that is set before us. Inspire us to run strong as we learn about all the saints that have gone before us. Give us endurance to be finishers of the race and not just beginners. Help us learn that the race of faith is a marathon and not a sprint. Teach us to be quick to let go of every kind of sin that would hold us back from running freely. Give us the focus to set our sights on you, Jesus, as the author and perfecter of our faith. Give us joy in you that captures our hearts and propels us forward in faith to do great things for your glory. May you be praised forever! In Jesus' name, amen.

Write down any thoughts you may want to *Share*:

DAY THREE // FAITH

Father, open my eyes that I might *see* you more clearly, *savor* you more fully, and *share* you more freely.

Circle or underline any key words or phrases you *See*:

You keep him in perfect peace whose mind is stayed on you, because he trusts in you. Trust in the LORD forever, for the LORD GOD is an everlasting rock. (Isaiah 26:3-4)

Savor these truths in prayer for yourself and others:

Father, your presence is a place of perfect peace where you keep those whose minds are focused on you. I pray that _____ and I would learn to fix our minds on you today with absolute trust. Give us a strong growing confidence in you that endures throughout our entire lives. Establish us in your perfect peace, knowing that you are our God and our everlasting rock. Give us the ability to see fear, worry, and anxiety as signals to turn to you in faith so that your perfect peace would reign in our hearts. Let our peace and faith in you give us the courage to love and care for the people that you bring into our lives. Cause us to know that you are the only trustworthy source in which we can place our faith. For your glory and our good, in Jesus' name, amen.

Write down any thoughts you may want to *Share*:

DAY FOUR // FAITH

Father, open my eyes that I might *see* you more clearly, *savor* you more fully, and *share* you more freely.

Circle or underline any key words or phrases you *See*:

And Jesus said to him, "If you can! All things are possible for one who believes." Immediately the father of the child cried out and said, "I believe; help my unbelief!" (Mark 9:23-24)

Savor these truths in prayer for yourself and others:

Father, thank you for the powerful promises you give us in your Word. Thank you for the hope that you offer to your children who trust you with their lives. I pray that you would give _____ and me the ability to see and feel our personal neediness for you in our lives. Give us eyes to see the beauty of your promises. Help us to know that feeling helpless can be one of your greatest gifts when we respond by calling out to you in humility for help. Teach us to know that all things are possible with you. Give us a daily desire to call out to you for more faith, "I believe! Help my unbelief!" Give us pleasure in trusting you in prayer. Use us to encourage others in pursuing you! For your glory and our good, in the faithful name of Jesus, amen.

Write down any thoughts you may want to *Share*:

DAY FIVE // FAITH

Father, open my eyes that I might *see* you more clearly, *savor* you more fully, and *share* you more freely.

Circle or underline any key words or phrases you *See*:

To this end we always pray for you, that our God may make you worthy of his calling and may fulfill every resolve for good and every work of faith by his power, so that the name of our Lord Jesus may be glorified in you, and you in him, according to the grace of our God and the Lord Jesus Christ. (2 Thessalonians 1:11-12)

Savor these truths in prayer for yourself and others:

Father, I pray for _____ and myself today, that you would show us your goodness in giving us a calling in our lives. Help us to know you are working in and through us to accomplish the things we are willing to trust you for. Teach us that every act of faith brings glory to your name because of your empowering grace. Help us find great joy in knowing that you are always with us, making us worthy of your calling on our lives. May the world know that we are your precious and loved children as we trust you each day. For your glory and our good, in Jesus' name, amen.

Write down any thoughts you may want to *Share*:

DAY SIX // FAITH

Father, open my eyes that I might *see* you more clearly, *savor* you more fully, and *share* you more freely.

Circle or underline any key words or phrases you *See*:

Fight the good fight of the faith. Take hold of the eternal life to which you were called and about which you made the good confession in the presence of many witnesses. (1 Timothy 6:12)
I have fought the good fight, I have finished the race, I have kept the faith. Henceforth there is laid up for me the crown of righteousness... (2 Timothy 4:7-8)

Savor these truths in prayer for yourself and others:

Father, I pray that _____ and I would learn that following you is a fight of faith to believe your good and perfect promises over the deceptive promises of the world, the flesh, and the devil. Help us understand that eternal life is real. Give us a growing sense that being with you for all eternity is of utmost importance. Instill in us a desire to fight the good fight of faith with focus and persistence. Give us childlike faith that yields our hearts to you and the power of your Spirit to believe all that you have promised. Give us delight in the truth that you have prepared a place for us as our Savior, Redeemer, and King. May the promise of eternal life with you compel us to fight the good fight of faith. For your glory and our good. In Jesus' name, amen.

Write down any thoughts you may want to *Share*:

DAY SEVEN // FAITH

Father, open my eyes that I might *see* you more clearly, *savor* you more fully, and *share* you more freely.

Circle or underline any key words or phrases you *See*:

...and I pray that the sharing of your faith may become effective for the full knowledge of every good thing that is in us for the sake of Christ. (Philemon 1:6)

Savor these truths in prayer for yourself and others:

Father, I pray that _____ and I would fall more and more deeply in love with you. Cause our love for you to be strong so that we would freely and naturally share our faith with others. Give us joy in seeing others come to trust you alone with their salvation and every aspect of their lives. Cause us to understand that sharing our faith actually deepens it in you and your promises. As we share our faith, give us eyes to see your glory, steadfast love, and faithfulness all along the way. Establish in our hearts the full knowledge of every good thing that is ours because of Christ. Give us your favor as we speak on your behalf in this world. Soften the hearts of those who hear of your goodness through us. For your glory and our good, in Jesus' name, amen.

Write down any thoughts you may want to *Share*:

NOTES

THE CORE FOUR

....

PURITY

never would have imagined that a simple combination of short paragraphs could transform how I approached following Jesus, and especially my pursuit of a life of purity. Hover over these three excerpts by Blaise Pascal, C. S. Lewis, and John Piper:

Blaise Pascal, 1623-1662, French mathematician, physicist, inventor, writer, and Christian philosopher:

All men seek happiness. This is without exception. Whatever different means they employ, they all tend to this end. The cause of some going to war, and of others avoiding it, is the same desire in both, attended with different views. The will never takes the least step but to this object. This is the motive of every action of every man, even of those who hang themselves. Pascal's Pensees, translated by W. F. Trotter (New York: E. P. Dutton, 1958). Page 113.

C. S. Lewis, 1898-1963, novelist, poet, English professor at Oxford University, lay theologian, broadcaster, lecturer, and Christian apologist:

If there lurks in most modern minds the notion that to desire our own good and earnestly to hope for the enjoyment of it is a bad thing, I submit that this notion has crept in from Kant and the Stoics and is no part of the Christian faith. Indeed, if we consider the unblushing promises of reward and the staggering nature of the rewards promised in the Gospels, it would seem that Our Lord finds our desires not too strong, but too weak. We are half-hearted creatures, fooling about with drink and sex and ambition when infinite joy is offered us, like an ignorant child who wants to go on making mud pies in a slum because he cannot imagine what is meant by the offer of a holiday at the sea. We are far too easily pleased. The Weight of Glory and Other Addresses (Grand Rapids: Eerdmans, 1965). Pages 1, 2.

John Piper, pastor, teacher, Founder of Desiring God Ministries, author:

Sin is what you do when your heart is not satisfied with God. No one sins out of duty. We sin because it holds out some promise of happiness. That promise enslaves us until we believe that God is more to be desired than life itself (Psalm 63:3). Which means the power of sin's promise is broken by the power of God's. All that God promises to be for us in Jesus stands over and against what sin promises to be for us without him. Future Grace (Sisters: Multnomah Books, 1995). Pages 9, 10.

These three paragraphs have become revolutionary for me and I think they can for you as well. Let's consider three insights drawn from these wells of goodness:

1. All men seek happiness.
2. We are far too easily pleased.
3. Sin is what you do when your heart is not satisfied with God.

For a long time I thought that my desire for pleasure was bad and evil. Was it wrongly focused and wrongly applied? Yes. But was it wrong? No! Our desire for pleasure is not bad; in fact it is God-given! The problem comes from *what* we seek to satisfy our desire for pleasure in. Through the insights from those three excerpts along with core passages of Scripture, I began to see that my desire for pleasure did not need to be squelched, but rather stoked. I needed to glut my desires in the greatness of God and not in the small fleeting pleasures of sin. I love what Lewis says: "We are far too easily pleased." That was a great description of me for a chunk of my life and I have to daily fight for delight in Jesus. It is a fight, not because Jesus is not quite enough to satisfy my heart, but because I am so distracted by what I see. My heart constantly wants to settle for lesser things.

Here is a secret: At the heart of each of those three paragraphs is a truth articulated by John Piper that has stuck with me like superglue for many years: "Each of us wants to get as much pleasure as we can possibly get and keep it for as long as we possibly can." We might not say this out loud, but it is true. It is also true that only God can meet the desires of our hearts. In fact, he created us to find our greatest pleasures in him. "You make known to me the path of life; in your presence there is fullness of joy; at your right hand are pleasures forevermore" (Psalm 16:11). Only in the Lord's presence can we experience fullness and complete joy. Only at his right hand are there unending pleasures.

God has our best in mind so much so that he commands us to find our greatest satisfaction in Him. "And he said to him, 'You shall love the Lord your God with all your heart and with all your soul and with all your mind'" (Matthew 22:37). Our challenge when it comes to living a life of purity is how we go about satisfying the God-given desires of our hearts. We need our hearts set free from the fleeting pleasures of sin and from being "far too easily pleased."

Purity Spotlight

"Watch and pray that you may not enter into temptation. The spirit indeed is willing, but the flesh is weak" (Mark 14:38). Much of our ability to pursue purity comes from our preparation. Jesus tells us to watch and pray that we may not enter temptation. The way to head temptation off before it gains too much of our hearts is through prayer preparation.

The path to purity is putting your hope and faith in the promises of God. We all are pursuing promises of pleasure. The real question is whether the promises we are pursuing lead us to the all-satisfying greatness of God or to the fleeting pleasures of sin. I know it sounds simple, but the more you are able to identify the promises that have a hold on your heart, the more likely you will be able to flourish in your life with God.

When you think about purity, it is also important to remember that there are no outward acts of impurity that do not start in the mind first. This is one of the reasons God encourages us to take every thought captive. Hover over these passages and let their truth and goodness saturate your heart and mind:

> *I appeal to you therefore, brothers, by the mercies of God, to present your bodies as a living sacrifice, holy and acceptable to God, which is your spiritual worship. Do not be conformed to this world, but be transformed by the renewal of your mind, that by testing you may discern what is the will of God, what is good and acceptable and perfect.* (Romans 12:1, 2)

> *How can a young man keep his way pure? By guarding it according to your word. With my whole heart I seek you; let me not wander from your*

commandments! I have stored up your word in my heart, that I might not sin against you. (Psalm 119:9-11)

"Blessed are the pure in heart, for they shall see God" (Matthew 5:8). Sometimes when I've read this passage I have felt hopeless and here's why: I know I don't have a pure heart, so seeing God seemed like an impossible dream. But here is an amazing truth—there are two kinds of purity: practical purity and positional purity. Positional purity means that God has made us pure in Christ. Jesus' sacrifice on the cross paid the penalty for our sins and makes us pure in the sight of God when we place our faith in Jesus as our savior and Lord. "For our sake he made him to be sin who knew no sin, so that in him we might become the righteousness of God" (2 Corinthians 5:21). He took on our sin and we took on his righteousness—the great exchange. In that moment we became pure in the sight of God.

Then there is the real time practical purity that we are called to live out on a daily basis. "Keep your heart with all vigilance, for from it flow the springs of life" (Proverbs 4:23). One of the great lies of the enemy is that you are the only one who is dealing with the sin that you are struggling with. It is a LIE! If Satan can make you believe you are alone in your sin, you will have a tendency to give up. Don't believe it. Memorize the following passage to strengthen your faith and hope in God that you are not alone in your pursuit in purity:

No temptation has overtaken you that is not common to man. God is faithful, and he will not let you be tempted beyond your ability, but with the temptation he will also provide the way of escape, that you may be able to endure it. (1 Corinthians 10:13)

Pray on!

WEEK FIVE // PRAYING FOR PURITY

If we don't feel strong desires for the manifestation of the glory of God, it is not because we have drunk deeply and are satisfied. It is because we have nibbled so long at the table of the world. Our soul is stuffed with small things, and there is no room for the great. — John Piper

DAY ONE // PURITY

Father, open my eyes that I might *see* you more clearly, *savor* you more fully, and *share* you more freely.

Circle or underline any key words or phrases you *See*:

No temptation has overtaken you that is not common to man. God is faithful, and he will not let you be tempted beyond your ability, but with the temptation he will also provide the way of escape, that you may be able to endure it. (1 Corinthians 10:13)

Savor these truths in prayer for yourself and others:

Father, thank you for the reminder that the temptations that we face are common to all mankind. The enemy of our souls wants us to believe that we are alone in our sin and temptations, but you have assured us that this is not the case. I pray that _____ and I would know that our temptations are not unique to us. Reassure us that you will help us overcome them. Give us faith to believe your promise that you will not allow us to be tempted beyond our ability. Don't let us forget that your promise of success is accompanied by a call to endure. Forge in us a faith that depends completely on the power of your Spirit. For your glory and our good, in Jesus' name, amen.

Write down any thoughts you may want to *Share*:

DAY TWO // PURITY

Father, open my eyes that I might *see* you more clearly, *savor* you more fully, and *share* you more freely.

Circle or underline any key words or phrases you *See*:

For this is the will of God, your sanctification: that you abstain from sexual immorality; that each one of you know how to control his body in holiness and honor, not in the passion of lust like the Gentiles who do not know God...For God has not called us for impurity, but in holiness. Therefore whoever disregards this, disregards not man but God, who gives his Holy Spirit to you. (1 Thessalonians 4:3-5, 7-8)

Savor these truths in prayer for yourself and others:

Father, thank you for making your will for our lives known. It is your will that we be sanctified or made holy specifically in our sexual relationships. I pray that you would empower _____ and me to abstain from all sexual immorality. Protect us in our personal relationships and guard our eyes against anything that would promote or demonstrate immoral relationships. Protect us from the devastating lure of lust. Give us discernment and desire for purity, and create seriousness in our hearts concerning how we control our bodies. Father, our holiness is serious to you because you are holy. Help us to embrace the truth that to disregard your calling on our lives for purity is to disregard you. For your glory and our good, in Jesus' name, amen.

Write down any thoughts you may want to *Share*:

71

DAY THREE // PURITY

Father, open my eyes that I might *see* you more clearly, *savor* you more fully, and *share* you more freely.

Circle or underline any key words or phrases you *See*:

Do not love the world or the things in the world. If anyone loves the world, the love of the Father is not in him. For all that is in the world—the desires of the flesh and the desires of the eyes and pride of life—is not from the Father but is from the world. And the world is passing away along with its desires, but whoever does the will of God abides forever. (1 John 2:15-17)

Savor these truths in prayer for yourself and others:

Father, you are clear in what is good for us and what is not. Too often our appetites lead us astray. I pray that you would give _____ and me appetites that cause supreme delight and enjoyment in you. Keep earthly loves from creeping into our hearts. Grant us an acute awareness of when we are being lured into the desires of the flesh. Give us eyes to see the futility in loving the things of this world. Cause our love for you to increase and abound in depth, breadth, length, and height. For your glory and our good. In Jesus' name, amen.

Write down any thoughts you may want to *Share*:

DAY FOUR // PURITY

Father, open my eyes that I might *see* you more clearly, *savor* you more fully, and *share* you more freely.

Circle or underline any key words or phrases you *See*:

Now to him who is able to keep you from stumbling and to present you blameless before the presence of his glory with great joy, to the only God, our Savior, through Jesus Christ our Lord, be glory, majesty, dominion, and authority, before all time and now and forever. Amen. (Jude 1:24-25)

Savor these truths in prayer for yourself and others:

Father, I commit _____ and myself to you today. You alone are able to keep us from stumbling and make us blameless in your presence. Don't let us get sidetracked by sin and temptation. Capture our minds and hearts with the wonder of one day entering into the presence of your glory. Cause us to move steadily toward you and your purposes. Make us long for you and your presence. May your name be blessed and praised forever. In Jesus' name, amen.

Write down any thoughts you may want to *Share*:

DAY FIVE // PURITY

Father, open my eyes that I might *see* you more clearly, *savor* you more fully, and *share* you more freely.

Circle or underline any key words or phrases you *See*:

Create in me a clean heart, O God, and renew a right spirit within me. Cast me not away from your presence, and take not your Holy Spirit from me. Restore to me the joy of your salvation, and uphold me with a willing spirit. (Psalm 51:10-12)

Savor these truths in prayer for yourself and others:

Father, only you can create a clean heart and renew a right spirit within us. Cause _____ and me to be discontented until we have come to you, so that you can cleanse our hearts and renew a right spirit within us. Help us to feel the weight of our disobedience toward you. Please do not let us become comfortable with unconfessed sin in our lives. Give us a longing to be in your presence. Help us to know the Holy Spirit's leading and conviction. Grant that we would desire more than anything the restoration of the joy of your salvation. May we rejoice in the sustaining power of your Spirit. For your glory and our good, in Jesus' name, amen.

Write down any thoughts you may want to *Share*:

DAY SIX // PURITY

Father, open my eyes that I might *see* you more clearly, *savor* you more fully, and *share* you more freely.

Circle or underline any key words or phrases you *See*:

Now may the God of peace himself sanctify you completely, and may your whole spirit and soul and body be kept blameless at the coming of our Lord Jesus Christ. He who calls you is faithful; he will surely do it. Brothers, pray for us. (1 Thessalonians 5:23-25)

Savor these truths in prayer for yourself and others:

Father, I praise you as the God of Peace. I call upon you to sanctify _____ and me completely. Please keep our whole spirit and body blameless before you. I stand in awe of your perfect faithfulness to us, your children. Thank you that you finish your work in each one of us. Don't let us wander from the truth, and help us yield to your will daily. May you enable us to embrace the sanctification process, letting go of sin and the weights that hold us back. Cause us to move forward, filled with your powerful peace. For your glory and our good, in Jesus' name, amen.

Write down any thoughts you may want to *Share*:

DAY SEVEN // PURITY

Father, open my eyes that I might *see* you more clearly, *savor* you more fully, and *share* you more freely.

Circle or underline any key words or phrases you *See:*

Every way of a man is right in his own eyes, but the LORD weighs the heart. (Proverbs 21:2)

All the ways of a man are pure in his own eyes, but the LORD weighs the spirit. (Proverbs 16:2)

The heart is deceitful above all things, and desperately sick; who can understand it? "I the LORD search the heart and test the mind..." (Jeremiah 17:9-10)

Savor these truths in prayer for yourself and others:

Father, ever since we turned from you in the garden we have thought that our way was the best way. Your way is always best. Forgive us for being deceived in thinking that our way is ever better than yours. I pray today that _____ and I would know the truth about our hearts. Cause us to walk humbly with you, the one who knows and understands our inmost thoughts and intentions. Transform our hearts to be in tune with you and your purposes, making them tender and teachable towards you and others. Cause us to submit to your Spirit and your Word, guiding and directing us in the way we should go. For your glory and our good, in Jesus' name, amen.

Write down any thoughts you may want to *Share:*

NOTES

THE PR (PUBLIC RELATIONS) PAIR

....

SPEECH

I love watching the award-winning specials produced by National Geographic. The eye-popping photography of nature that they are able to capture is stunning. I am specifically reminded of a photograph of an iceberg in Pleneau Bay off Pleneau Island, which for those of us who are geographically challenged, is close to the Antarctic Circle at the bottom of the world. The photograph was a split shot view capturing a unique image of the iceberg both above and below the waterline. This picture brought the phrase "tip of the iceberg" to life for me. Scientists state that because of the density of ice, only ten percent of an iceberg is visible above water, while the bulk of its substance sits below the surface. When you think about it, we are actually a lot like icebergs. People around us get to see about ten percent of who we really are through our speech and conduct, but there is so much more to us that is under the waterline. In some ways, our speech and conduct are like high-tech animated billboards above the surface sending messages to all who pass by saying, "This is who I am!" Like all messages from billboards, our speech and conduct only serve as signs of who we are below the surface. They give clues, but they don't share the whole story. They are just the tip of the iceberg.

It is in our speech and conduct that we go public with who we are, or at least who we want people to *think* we are, on the inside.

Our wisdom, love, faith, and purity are forged on the inside and then expressed on the outside in what we say and do. This is where the rubber meets the road in our Christian lives. The importance of our speech and conduct cannot be overstated. The goal is for what we say and do to accurately reflect who we are on the inside. As followers of Jesus it is through what we say and do that we offer the world either a clear or hazy picture of who God is. We were created by God to magnify his greatness by our lips and by our lives.

I want to challenge you with two simple questions to help guide you in becoming an authentic follower of Christ in both your speech and conduct. These questions are designed to shine a light on the state of your hearts and to direct you toward an ever-increasing dependence on God.

1. *Am I playing the part without the heart?* God's greatest desire for us is that we would love him with all our heart, soul, mind, and strength, and that we would love others as ourselves. This question points to our tendency to pretend that he is our treasure when other things are really our pleasure. Jesus saved some of his most scathing words for those who honored him with their lips while their hearts were far from him. Let this question do its good work and prompt us toward having a heart that is captured by God and his greatness.

2. *Am I allowing my speech and conduct to fulfill their purpose in my spiritual growth?* Our speech and conduct serve these purposes: to communicate to the world who we are and what we stand for, and to communicate with ourselves. Are you listening to what your speech and conduct are telling you about the spiritual condition of your heart?

As followers of Christ, we have the Holy Spirit living in us helping us know when we say or do something that is out of sync with either who we are or who God calls us to be in his Word. It is crucial that we listen to the Spirit's convictions and promptings. We must be careful not to resist and quench the Holy Spirit's working within us. We must listen to the Holy Spirit when he brings our sin and inconsistencies to light and respond by confessing and forsaking them by his power. This is one of the key ways we are conformed to the image of Jesus, which is God's ultimate purpose for our lives.

....

Even a fool who keeps silent is considered wise; when he closes his lips, he is deemed intelligent. (Proverbs 17:28)

When words are many, transgression is not lacking, but whoever restrains his lips is prudent. (Proverbs 10:19)

Know this, my beloved brothers: let every person be quick to hear, slow to speak, slow to anger; for the anger of man does not produce the righteousness of God. (James 1:19)

It is not a mistake that I introduce the speech section using passages that focus on silence and the hazards associated with too many words. I love the old saying that goes something like this: "God has given you two ears and one mouth so be sure to listen twice as much as you speak."

Our speech is serious business. The challenge to be careful in how we speak hit home for me in a powerful way when I came across this passage: "I tell you, on the day of judgment people will give account for every careless word they speak, for by your words you will be justified, and by your words you will be condemned"

(Matthew 12:36-37). It makes sense that our words affect our eternity when we realize that it is with our mouths that we confess what we believe about Jesus. It is also with our mouths that we call out to Jesus for salvation. Take a look at Romans 10:8-13:

> ..."The word is near you, in your mouth and in your heart" (that is, the word of faith that we proclaim); because, if you confess with your mouth that Jesus is Lord and believe in your heart that God raised him from the dead, you will be saved. For with the heart one believes and is justified, and with the mouth one confesses and is saved. For the Scripture says, "Everyone who believes in him will not be put to shame." For there is no distinction between Jew and Greek; for the same Lord is Lord of all, bestowing his riches on all who call on him. For "everyone who calls on the name of the Lord will be saved."

Pray on!

WEEK SIX // PRAYING FOR SPEECH

The Bible gives us enormous understanding concerning the power of our speech. Hover over these passages as you prepare to pray about speech, and make a commitment to use your words to bring life, healing, and gladness:

The good person out of the good treasure of his heart produces good, and the evil person out of his evil treasure produces evil, for out of the abundance of the heart his mouth speaks. (Luke 6:45)

Death and life are in the power of the tongue, and those who love it will eat its fruits. (Proverbs 18:21)

There is one whose rash words are like sword thrusts, but the tongue of the wise brings healing. (Proverbs 12:18)

Anxiety in a man's heart weighs him down, but a good word makes him glad. (Proverbs 12:25)

DAY ONE // SPEECH

Father, open my eyes that I might *see* you more clearly, *savor* you more fully, and *share* you more freely.

Circle or underline any key words or phrases you *See*:

Let no corrupting talk come out of your mouths, but only such as is good for building up, as fits the occasion, that it may give grace to those who hear. (Ephesians 4:29)
Let there be no filthiness nor foolish talk nor crude joking, which are out of place, but instead let there be thanksgiving. (Ephesians 5:4)

Savor these truths in prayer for yourself and others:

Father, we live in a world that is so often careless and crude in how we use our speech. I pray that you would pro-tect _____ and me from speech that can corrupt and tear us down. Help us to see destructive speech and never become comfortable with it from our friends or from our-selves. Give us a strong desire and determination to only use words that encourage others. Help us to learn to speak good words with purpose and precision. Guard us from speech that is filled with filthiness and crude joking. Help us to learn to initiate conversations that are gracious, en-couraging, and filled with gratefulness for all that you have done for us. Make thankfulness our primary way we battle speech around us that is filled with filthiness, foolishness, or crude joking, so that you are glorified and others are up-lifted. For your glory and our good, in Jesus' name, amen.

Write down any thoughts you may want to *Share*:

DAY TWO // SPEECH

Father, open my eyes that I might *see* you more clearly, *savor* you more fully, and *share* you more freely.

Circle or underline any key words or phrases you *See*:

...do not be anxious about anything, but in everything by prayer and supplication with thanksgiving let your requests be made known to God. And the peace of God, which surpasses all understanding, will guard your hearts and your minds in Christ Jesus. (Philippians 4:6-7)

Savor these truths in prayer for yourself and others:

Father, there is so much in life that is out of our control which can lead to fear and anxiety. Thank you that you are sufficient for all things in our lives and that there is nothing outside of your control. I pray that _____ and I would learn to place our hope and trust in you in all circumstances. Cause our natural response to uncertainty to be prayer that is filled with thanksgiving to Jesus as the one who holds all things together by the power of his Word. Make your promise of peace surpass all our understanding when we pray, flooding our hearts and minds in Christ. Make fear or anxiety flee our hearts and minds, as we trust you in prayer. Help us learn to offer prayers that are saturated with thanksgiving for all that you are. Cause us to learn to pray without ceasing, making it our most-used form of speech. For your glory and our good, in Jesus' name, amen.

Write down any thoughts you may want to *Share*:

DAY THREE // SPEECH

Father, open my eyes that I might *see* you more clearly, *savor* you more fully, and *share* you more freely.

Circle or underline any key words or phrases you *See*:

Continue steadfastly in prayer, being watchful in it with thanksgiving. At the same time, pray also for us, that God may open to us a door for the word, to declare the mystery of Christ, on account of which I am in prison—that I may make it clear, which is how I ought to speak. (Colossians 4:2-4)

Savor these truths in prayer for yourself and others:

Father, thank you for the gift of being able to talk to you in prayer. It is my hope and prayer for _____ and myself today that speaking to you in prayer would become as natural as breathing. Just as breathing sustains our physical lives, help us understand that steadfastness in prayer sustains our relationship with you. Help us to learn to be alert to the needs for prayer around us. Give us so much confidence and hope in you that all of our prayers would have a flavor of worship and thankfulness. I pray specifically that you would grow our desire to see the mystery of Christ proclaimed. Give us the willingness and ability to share the wonders of what you have done in Christ freely and frequently. Grant that we would not only share your greatness clearly and simply but that we would help others find freedom in sharing you as well. For your glory and our good, in Jesus' name, amen.

Write down any thoughts you may want to *Share*:

DAY FOUR // SPEECH

Father, open my eyes that I might *see* you more clearly, *savor* you more fully, and *share* you more freely.

Circle or underline any key words or phrases you *See:*

Let your speech always be gracious, seasoned with salt, so that you may know how you ought to answer each person. (Colossians 4:6)

Savor these truths in prayer for yourself and others:

Father, I pray today that you would bless _____ and me with your favor and wisdom especially in how we talk with others. Give us gracious speech. Teach us that gracious speech is humble speech and is not boastful or proud. Help us learn to help others flourish in life with the words we speak. Create in us speech that is gracious and seasoned with your wisdom so that we will know how to answer everyone who engages with us. Cause us to become magnets for good conversations that build others up and that honor you. Give us friends who also desire to speak words that are gracious and encouraging. May the words we speak be used to create a hunger and thirst for you and your truth. For your glory and our good, in Jesus' name, amen.

Write down any thoughts you may want to *Share:*

DAY FIVE // SPEECH

Father, open my eyes that I might *see* you more clearly, *savor* you more fully, and *share* you more freely.

Circle or underline any key words or phrases you *See*:

Have nothing to do with foolish, ignorant controversies; you know that they breed quarrels. And the Lord's servant must not be quarrelsome but kind to everyone, able to teach, patiently enduring evil, correcting his opponents with gentleness. God may perhaps grant them repentance leading to a knowledge of the truth... (2 Timothy 2:23-25)

Savor these truths in prayer for yourself and others:

Father, I pray that you would protect _____ and me today from foolish speech. It is so easy to be proud and engage in arguments that do not even matter. Give us wisdom to know when a pointless argument is starting up in conversation and help us learn to become peacemakers when quarrels erupt. I pray that you would fill us with your kindness and patience in all our conversations. Give us the ability to teach others about you in a gentle and loving way so that perhaps they might turn to you in faith believing the truth. Give us a desire to please you with how we speak with others. May you be praised by all the gracious ways your children speak. In Jesus' name, amen.

Write down any thoughts you may want to *Share*:

DAY SIX // SPEECH

Father, open my eyes that I might *see* you more clearly, *savor* you more fully, and *share* you more freely.

Circle or underline any key words or phrases you *See*:

Rejoice always, pray without ceasing, give thanks in all circumstances; for this is the will of God in Christ Jesus for you. (1 Thessalonians 5:16-18)

We give thanks to God always for all of you, constantly mentioning you in our prayers... (1 Thessalonians 1:2)

Savor these truths in prayer for yourself and others:

Father, thank you for clearly revealing your will for us in Christ Jesus. I pray that _____ and I would have a lifestyle that is marked by rejoicing, prayer, and thankfulness. Cause us to find joy in your goodness each day, and help us to express that joy through praise to you. Create in us a longing to see your greatness each day, and help us express our longing in relentless prayer. Help our prayers to be saturated with thankfulness for all things in all circumstances. Give us eyes to see the good you are doing in and through others. Cause our hearts to overflow in thankfulness toward you. For your glory and our good, in Jesus' name, amen.

Write down any thoughts you may want to *Share*:

DAY SEVEN // SPEECH

Father, open my eyes that I might *see* you more clearly, *savor* you more fully, and *share* you more freely.

Circle or underline any key words or phrases you *See*:

Therefore God has highly exalted him and bestowed on him the name that is above every name, so that at the name of Jesus every knee should bow, in heaven and on earth and under the earth, and every tongue confess that Jesus Christ is Lord, to the glory of God the Father. (Philippians 2:9-11)

...for it is written, "As I live, says the Lord, every knee shall bow to me, and every tongue confess to God." (Romans 14:11)

Savor these truths in prayer for yourself and others:

Father, thank you that Jesus is Lord over all things and that you are highly exalted above all other competitors for your glory whether in heaven or on earth. I pray that you would help _____ and me see and savor your Lordship for all it is worth. Cause our hearts to grow in love and adoration for you as we learn more about your greatness. Help us understand that one day every knee everywhere will bow before your greatness. Give us understanding that every person on this planet will one day confess that Jesus is Lord and that confession will bring massive glory to you. Give us joy in telling our friends how great you are as we look to the day when everyone will sing your praises. For your glory and our good, in Jesus' name, amen.

Write down any thoughts you may want to *Share*:

NOTES

THE PR PAIR

....

CONDUCT

There is a plethora of things that could be said about living a God-honoring life, but in this case less is more. I will be using several passages from the Bible where God summarizes and clarifies what he desires from us along with some principles to help us flourish in following Jesus.

> And he said to him, "You shall love the Lord your God with all your heart and with all your soul and with all your mind. This is the great and first commandment. And a second is like it: You shall love your neighbor as yourself. On these two commandments depend all the Law and the Prophets. (Matthew 22:37-40)

When by the power of the Holy Spirit you let your conduct be saturated by love for God and others, you are satisfying all of the Law and the Prophets.

Years ago my wife put her artistic skills to work by stenciling what could be my all time favorite passage around the top of my office walls. It has given me more clarity into what drives my own heart as well as God's heart than any other single passage. Let's look at it in two parts so we can see how it unfolds:

(23) *Thus says the LORD: "Let not the wise man boast in his wisdom, let not the mighty man boast in his might, let not the rich man boast in his riches,*

(24) *but let him who boasts boast in this, that he understands and knows me, that I am the LORD who practices steadfast love, justice, and righteousness in the earth. For in these things I delight, declares the LORD."* (Jeremiah 9:23-24)

Verse 23 shines a light on what motivates us as humans. We are driven to boast and find our identity in our wisdom, strength, and riches, and this isn't surprising—from the beginning we've all tried to go our way like Adam and Eve when they disobeyed God (Genesis 3). Since then people have tried to use God's gifts of wisdom, strength, and riches to make a name for themselves (Genesis 11). God intends for these gifts to be used to make his name greater. Take a look at what happens when we try to use these gifts to magnify ourselves rather than God:

1. *Wisdom*: This is anything related to our intellect or insight. This is often seen in our academic pursuits or achieving a higher GPA, GRE or MCAT score. It could also be seen in our desire to be witty or clever.
2. *Strength*: This deals with physical strength or beauty. This doesn't take a lot of explanation. The air we breathe in our culture puts enormous emphasis on athletic prowess or the airbrushed complexions of the models on the magazine covers.
3. *Riches*: This creates pride or boasting in what we own or the position and prestige that wealth provides in society.

One way to know whether you are seeking to find your identity in any of these areas is through your desire for affirmation.

What is it that you want people to say about you if they were describing you to someone else? What are the compliments that you long to hear? I remember when I first saw this passage and started to process its implications. I felt exposed. I wanted all of these things. I wanted to be smart and make great grades even though it was a stretch. I wanted to be the star athlete and be good looking but I am DNA challenged in both of these arenas. Lastly, I wanted to get a great job and make lots of money. Well, at least I love my job. Then the light came on. God was not saying that we should not seek to excel in these three primary aspects of life. He was saying don't *boast* in them or don't try to find your *identity* in them. God knows we are wired to boast in something. He just doesn't want us to settle for boasting in these three areas. It's another case of C.S. Lewis' quote about our leanings to be "far too easily pleased".

Jeremiah 9:24 makes it clear that we should aim higher in our boasting and identity. God wants us to boast that we know him, which is a startling statement since his magnificence is unfathomable. Specifically, he wants us to boast that we know and understand what is on his heart and what he wants to accomplish on the earth. This passage reveals that God does three things on earth that he delights in: he practices steadfast love, justice, and righteousness. It is absolutely amazing that God has given us such a clear picture of what he delights to do and what he calls us to be about as well. Since God is the giver of wisdom, strength, and riches, he wants us to pursue those things—not for our sake, but for his glory. We should not pursue them to make a name for ourselves, but so that we can use them to advance his steadfast love, justice, and righteousness on the earth. This brings him great delight and us great joy.

SOUDER

Living a life in sync with the purposes of God is not easy. Loving people can be messy, but worth it. Thwarting injustice is hard. People who benefit from injustice of any kind do not want to lose those benefits. People who are unjust do not want to be called out and exposed in their evil. Advancing righteousness exposes un-righteousness and people tend to be resistant to this. BUT, it's all worth it when you know that your life and conduct are bringing delight to the heart of God, because he delights in practicing stead-fast love, justice, and righteousness on the earth.

If you want to gain clarity of purpose for your life, I encourage you to begin using Jeremiah 9:23-24 as a lens through which you view your life and actions. As you begin to live in a way that lines up with what God is doing on earth, your life will become more satisfying than you could ever imagine. As I began to hover over this passage more intently, I saw that the three things God does on the earth are the sum of the Gospel. The Gospel is God loving the world so much that he sent his son to satisfy his justice by paying for our sin and giving us Jesus' righteousness. May we join our heavenly Father in seeking to bring the Gospel to a hurting world as we practice steadfast love, thwart injustice, and advance righteousness.

Practically Speaking

Develop a healthy sense of accountability: Your life counts. The way you live matters, not only in relationship to God but also in its impact on others. Our lives are like a rock thrown in a lake, which disrupts the tranquility of the water and sends ripples expanding outward. Every act has an impact. It may not be as clear as the ripples from the splashing rock, but our actions make a difference. Most of us tend to live more thoughtful and powerful lives when we know we will have to give an account for what we've done. Also, having friends and adult mentors who will check in on you will help build external accountability into your life. Increase the people who are on your team and who help you to live the life you desire that pleases God. This will dramatically reduce the amount of regrets you have to carry into the future.

So teach us to number our days that we may get a heart of wisdom. (Psalm 90:12)

Look carefully then how you walk, not as unwise but as wise, making the best use of the time, because the days are evil. (Ephesians 5:15-16)

We all have a limited amount of time on this earth before we stand before God. He will hold us accountable for our lives. Numbering your days is a way to remind yourself that you only have a short time to make the most of your life. The result of learning to make every day count is a heart of wisdom.

On our last day we all want to hear "well done" from our heavenly Father. We may not be thinking about it now, but when the time comes there will be no other words that will be more valuable to us. May God grant each of us an unquenchable desire to hear him say "well done!"

Pray on!

WEEK SEVEN // PRAYING FOR CONDUCT

Whoever says "I know him" but does not keep his commandments is a liar, and the truth is not in him, but whoever keeps his word, in him truly the love of God is perfected. By this we may know that we are in him: whoever says he abides in him ought to walk in the same way in which he walked. (1 John 2:4-6)

DAY ONE // CONDUCT

Father, open my eyes that I might *see* you more clearly, *savor* you more fully, and *share* you more freely.

Circle or underline any key words or phrases you *See*:

I am the vine; you are the branches. Whoever abides in me and I in him, he it is that bears much fruit, for apart from me you can do nothing. (John 15:5)

Savor these truths in prayer for yourself and others:

Father, thank you that you are our great and glorious creator and sustainer. I pray that you would cause _____ and me to have a growing sense that our lives are yours and that we are dependent on you for everything. Give us eyes to see, ears to hear, and hearts that understand how your sustaining provision causes us to flourish when we hope and trust in you. Give us a desire to flourish in the way we live and thus a strong desire to abide and rest in you. Help us to know that apart from you we can do nothing. Don't let us be deceived into thinking that we can pull ourselves up by our own bootstraps. Give us a clear understanding that you are the one who gives us the strength to even put on our boots. Empower us by your Spirit to bear fruit that lasts. Give us a longing to abide in you and help others to come and find their greatest satisfaction in you. For your glory and our good, in Jesus' name, amen.

Write down any thoughts you may want to *Share*:

DAY TWO // CONDUCT

Father, open my eyes that I might *see* you more clearly, *savor* you more fully, and *share* you more freely.

Circle or underline any key words or phrases you *See*:

Therefore, since we have been justified by faith, we have peace with God through our Lord Jesus Christ. Through him we have also obtained access by faith into this grace in which we stand, and we rejoice in hope of the glory of God. Not only that, but rejoice in our sufferings, knowing that suffering produces endurance, and endurance produces character, and character produces hope, and hope does not put us to shame, because God's love has been poured into our hearts through the Holy Spirit who has been given to us. (Romans 5:1-5)

Savor these truths in prayer for yourself and others:

Father, I praise you for your great work in _____ and me today. Bless us today with a growing understanding of the wonder of your grace that makes it possible for us to know you through Jesus. Give us grace to know that every trial we face has a purpose that is often bigger than what we can see. By your mercy help us to see glimpses of the character and hope you are forging in our lives. Cause us to see and savor the lavish love you have poured into our hearts by the Holy Spirit. Fill our hearts and mouths with praise for all of the goodness that results from enduring through hardships. May our hope in you always propel us forward in faith. For your glory and our good, in Jesus' name, amen.

Write down any thoughts you may want to *Share*:

DAY THREE // CONDUCT

Father, open my eyes that I might *see* you more clearly, *savor* you more fully, and *share* you more freely.

Circle or underline any key words or phrases you *See*:

His master said to him, 'Well done, good and faithful servant. You have been faithful over a little; I will set you over much. Enter into the joy of your master.' (Matthew 25:21)

For we are his workmanship, created in Christ Jesus for good works which God prepared beforehand, that we should walk in them. (Ephesians 2:10)

Savor these truths in prayer for yourself and others:

Father, thank you that you have created _____ and me for your glory. Thank you for the natural abilities and specific personalities you have given us to accomplish your purposes. I pray that we would long to fulfill those purposes and please you. Give us a tenacity of purpose and joy that is fueled by your love for us. Cause us to live faithfully for you even when it is hard, knowing that we are your workmanship, created in Christ Jesus to make a lasting difference in this world. Help us to start our journey of faith with you well, but more importantly I pray that you would empower us to finish well. Give us strength to persevere so that we hear your marvelous words: "Well done, good and faithful servant" and "Enter into the joy of your master." For your glory and our good, in Jesus' name, amen.

Write down any thoughts you may want to *Share*:

DAY FOUR // CONDUCT

Father, open my eyes that I might *see* you more clearly, *savor* you more fully, and *share* you more freely.

Circle or underline any key words or phrases you *See*:

You are the light of the world. A city set on a hill cannot be hidden. Nor do people light a lamp and put it under a basket, but on a stand, and it gives light to all in the house. In the same way, let your light shine before others, so that they may see your good works and give glory to your Father who is in heaven. (Matthew 5:14-16)

Savor these truths in prayer for yourself and others:

Father, you have called us to shine in such a way that the world will know you are great. I pray that _____ and I would grow in our understanding that our life's purpose is to show how great you are. Protect us from a spirit of fear that would cause us to hide our light behind shyness. Create in us courage to do works of love, kindness, mercy, and justice so that the world might be drawn to the beauty of Jesus. Make us bold for your glory. Give us a clear sense of the presence of the Holy Spirit working in us to make Jesus known to the world. Bless us with understanding of how to serve you and others that would help us to trust you with our lives. Let us also help others find the joy of serving and glorifying you through their good works. May you be praised forever, in Jesus' name, amen.

Write down any thoughts you may want to *Share*:

DAY FIVE // CONDUCT

Father, open my eyes that I might *see* you more clearly, *savor* you more fully, and *share* you more freely.

Circle or underline any key words or phrases you *See*:

Live in harmony with one another. Do not be haughty, but associate with the lowly. Never be wise in your own sight. Repay no one evil for evil, but give thought to do what is honorable in the sight of all. If possible, so far as it depends on you, live peaceably with all. (Romans 12:16-18)

Savor these truths in prayer for yourself and others:

Father, you are worthy of all praise and sacrifice. All of your commands are designed for our good. Thank you for the admonitions in this passage that show us how to live a life that flourishes with others. I pray that _____ and I would find joy in pursuing a life of harmony with others. Protect us from ever thinking that we are better than others. Give us eyes to see when we are beginning to become haughty and proud. Cause us to feel freedom in engaging with those who are less fortunate, knowing that everything we have is by your gracious hand. Create in us the character of Christ that is full of forgiveness. Give us the power of your spirit to do what is honorable in the sight of all, just as Jesus did when he unjustly suffered. Create in us a passionate desire to live at peace with everyone. For your glory and our good, in Jesus' name, amen.

Write down any thoughts you may want to *Share*:

DAY SIX // CONDUCT

Father, open my eyes that I might *see* you more clearly, *savor* you more fully, and *share* you more freely.

Circle or underline any key words or phrases you *See*:

So whether you eat or drink, or whatever you do, do all to the glory of God. (1 Corinthians 10:31)
And whatever you do, in word or deed, do everything in the name of the Lord Jesus, giving thanks to God the Father through him. (Colossians 3:17)

Savor these truths in prayer for yourself and others:

Father, thank you that our lives belong to you. You created _____ and me by your power and for your glory. It is only when we live for your glory that our lives can be fulfilled. I pray that you would draw us to yourself today so we would know the sweetness and power of your presence. I ask that you would give us strength, desire, and passion to do everything we do today for your glory. Help us to give thanks to you in all things. Develop within us an amazingly thankful spirit. Cause us to enjoy each moment of our lives, knowing that they are gifts from you. Make our hearts overflow with thankfulness to you in all we say and do, reminding us that you are the provider of all things. May your name be exalted by whatever we do today. For your glory and our good, in Jesus' name, amen.

Write down any thoughts you may want to *Share*:

DAY SEVEN // CONDUCT

Father, open my eyes that I might *see* you more clearly, *savor* you more fully, and *share* you more freely.

Circle or underline any key words or phrases you *See*:

But exhort one another every day, as long as it is called "today," that none of you may be hardened by the deceitfulness of sin. (Hebrews 3:13)

Savor these truths in prayer for yourself and others:

Father, thank you that you do not let us just go our own way. Thank you that you care and correct us through your Word. Your correction is a demonstration of your great love for us. I pray that you would raise up friends in our lives who will hold us accountable. Help us to realize that loving correction is a gift from you that helps protect us from sin. Give us the ability to spot deception and create in us eyes to see the deceitfulness of sin. Give us tender and responsive hearts when we are confronted with an area of sin in our lives. Keep us from rebelling against the people in our lives who challenge us with the truth, and protect us from hardening our hearts to that truth. For your glory and our good, in Jesus' name, amen.

Write down any thoughts you may want to *Share*:

NOTES

PART THREE

....

31-DAY CYCLE OF PRAYERS

O ver the next 31 days you'll have the opportunity to really start experiencing the rhythm of praying Scripture over yourself and your friends.

We want this 31-day cycle of prayers to be a resource for you even within the prayer guide. If we are honest with ourselves, there are moments when we don't know how to pray, what to pray, or we simply cannot find the desire to do so. In those moments, do not feel defeated. Instead, on that 7th day of the month when your prayer guide has laid on your bedside table untouched since the month started, pick it up and turn to day 7 in the 31-day cycle and pray that prayer for yourself and your peers. Let us remember and be grateful that God's willingness to hear us is not dependent on the temperature of our hearts when we approach him.

You've gone through The 7 Essentials, and now you have a chance to expand on them. Take notes along the way, make the prayers your own, and enjoy your next month-long journey!

SOUDER

DAY ONE // FAVOR

Father, open my eyes that I might *see* you more clearly, *savor* you more fully, and *share* you more freely.

Circle or underline any key words or phrases you *See*:

Yours, O LORD, is the greatness and the power and the glory and the victory and the majesty, for all that is in the heavens and in the earth is yours. Yours is the kingdom, O LORD, and you are exalted as head above all. Both riches and honor come from you, and you rule over all. In your hand are power and might, and in your hand it is to make great and to give strength to all. And now we thank you, our God, and praise your glorious name. (1 Chronicles 29:11-13)

Savor these truths in prayer for yourself and others:

Father, you are great and worthy to be praised. I pray that you would give your boundless favor to _____ and me, so that we may have eyes to see your greatness, power, and glory in all creation. Awaken our hearts and minds to begin understanding your faithfulness in our lives as Lord over all things. When we look at the sky above, cause us to know the heavens are yours! When we look in the mirror, cause us to know that we are yours. Create in us an unceasing reliance on you and your provisions of favor each day. May we continually become more enthralled by your greatness, causing our hearts to overflow with thankfulness at every thought of you. For your glory and our good, in the sovereign name of Jesus, amen.

Write down any thoughts you may want to *Share*:

DAY TWO // WISDOM

Father, open my eyes that I might *see* you more clearly, *savor* you more fully, and *share* you more freely.

Circle or underline any key words or phrases you *See*:

So teach us to number our days that we may get a heart of wisdom. (Psalm 90:12)
O Lord, make me know my end and what is the measure of my days; let me know how fleeting I am! (Psalm 39:4)

Savor these truths in prayer for yourself and others:

Father, it is so easy for days and years to pass by before we realize they are gone. I pray that _____ and I would learn the importance of a single day. Teach us to savor the moments of every day as special gifts from you. As we learn to number our days, cause our hearts and minds to overflow with your deep and practical wisdom. Cause us to grow into adults who love you and bless others because we understand your sustaining love in our lives. Help us to realize this life is fleeting and that there is no time to waste in helping others see and savor your greatness. Give us a long-term view of life so we can make wise short-term decisions. Remind us that it is in living for you that our lives become the most fulfilling. For your glory and our good, in Jesus' name, amen.

Write down any thoughts you may want to *Share*:

DAY THREE // LOVE

Father, open my eyes that I might *see* you more clearly, *savor* you more fully, and *share* you more freely.

Circle or underline any key words or phrases you *See*:

For God so loved the world, that he gave his only Son, that whoever believes in him should not perish but have eternal life. (John 3:16)

For while we were still weak, at the right time Christ died for the ungodly. For one will scarcely die for a righteous person—though perhaps for a good person one would dare even to die—but God shows his love for us in that while we were still sinners, Christ died for us. (Romans 5:6-8)

Savor these truths in prayer for yourself and others:

Father, thank you that the magnitude of your love is seen in the life, death, and resurrection of your Son, Jesus. I pray that you would give _____ and me eyes to see that your amazing love displayed in Jesus has overcome all the sin that has separated us from you as our creator. Help us to understand that your love for us in Jesus is a gift of grace and cannot be earned or deserved. Give us a clear sense of what sin is and how it separates us from you and from others. Give us faith to trust in Jesus alone to restore our relationship with you. For your glory and our good, in Jesus' name, amen.

Write down any thoughts you may want to *Share*:

DAY FOUR // FAITH

Father, open my eyes that I might *see* you more clearly, *savor* you more fully, and *share* you more freely.

Circle or underline any key words or phrases you *See*:

Trust in the LORD with all your heart, and do not lean on your own understanding. In all your ways acknowledge him, and he will make straight your paths. (Proverbs 3:5-6)

Savor these truths in prayer for yourself and others:

Father, life is so often complex and confusing. I thank you for your promises that provide hope and clarity in the midst of life's complexity. Today I pray that _____ and I would place our trust in you. Help us learn to surrender our lives to you, knowing how much you love us. Empower us to fight the urge to rely on our own understanding more than we rely on you and your guidance. Make our hearts tender towards you and your purposes so that it becomes as natural as breathing for us to look to you in all our ways. Help us to recognize and acknowledge all of your provisions as we see you make our paths straight. You are our God! Help us to treasure you today with every breath, and cause us to encourage others to treasure you with all of their hearts as well. For your glory and our good, in Jesus' name, amen.

Write down any thoughts you may want to *Share*:

DAY FIVE // PURITY

Father, open my eyes that I might *see* you more clearly, *savor* you more fully, and *share* you more freely.

Circle or underline any key words or phrases you *See*:

How can a young man keep his way pure? By guarding it according to your word. With my whole heart I seek you; let me not wander from your commandments! I have stored up your word in my heart, that I might not sin against you. (Psalm 119:9-11)

Savor these truths in prayer for yourself and others:

Father, in a world that disregards purity, the question of the psalmist is vital: "How can a young man [or woman] keep their way pure?" A wholehearted pursuit of you and your Word is the answer. I pray that _____ and I would taste the sweetness of Scripture and desire it with our whole hearts. Help us to believe that your Word is the Sword of the Spirit that can lead, guide, and empower us to pursue purity in every decision. Give us the desire and will to hide your Word in our hearts that we might not sin against you. Holy, holy, holy is the Lord God Almighty. In Jesus' name, amen.

Write down any thoughts you may want to *Share*:

DAY SIX // SPEECH

Father, open my eyes that I might *see* you more clearly, *savor* you more fully, and *share* you more freely.

Circle or underline any key words or phrases you *See*:

It is good to give to thanks to the LORD, to sing praises to your name, O Most High; to declare your steadfast love in the morning, and your faithfulness by night... (Psalm 92:1-2)

Savor these truths in prayer for yourself and others:

Father, I praise you today. You are great and glorious. Help ________ and me to use our words to give you thanks for all you are and all you do. Give us joy in you so that our hearts overflow with songs of praise to your name. Help us to have a growing awareness of your great love for us each morning. Give us the ability to recognize your faithfulness throughout each day. Help us learn to not only see your deep and abiding love and faithfulness, but to soak it in and savor each aspect of your goodness. May our seeing and savoring overflow into learning how to naturally share our thankfulness for your goodness. Give us mentors and models who can show us what it means to love and adore you with thankfulness and praise. For your glory and our good, in Jesus' name, amen.

Write down any thoughts you may want to *Share*:

DAY SEVEN // CONDUCT

Father, open my eyes that I might *see* you more clearly, *savor* you more fully, and *share* you more freely.

Circle or underline any key words or phrases you *See*:

He has told you, O man, what is good; and what does the LORD require of you but to do justice, and to love kindness, and to walk humbly with your God? (Micah 6:8)

Savor these truths in prayer for yourself and others:

Father, thank you for telling us what is good in this life along with the things you require of us to honor your name. I pray that _____ and I would learn to love what you require of us. Make our hearts tender and responsive to all of your commands to do justice, love kindness, and walk humbly with you all of our days. Awaken our hearts and minds to the needs for love and mercy all around us and give us the wisdom, abilities, and tenacious desire required to meet those needs. Give us eyes to see the world the way you see it and grant us courage to stand against injustice for your glory and the good of those being mistreated. As we seek to promote justice and to love kindness in this world, empower us to do it with humility before you and man. For your glory and our good, in Jesus' name, amen.

Write down any thoughts you may want to *Share*:

NOTES

One of the beautiful aspects of prayer is that it is not just one directional. It is not just a cathartic experience where we unload on God to feel better. God communicates to us when we pray if we pause long enough to listen. God uses his Word and his Spirit to bring guidance, understanding, and conviction. You can be sure that he will never bring something to mind that is contrary to his Word. So ask him for guidance, understanding, and even conviction concerning anything in your world that needs to be addressed. Don't be afraid—he wants the best for you.

....

DAY EIGHT // FAVOR

Father, open my eyes that I might *see* you more clearly, *savor* you more fully, and *share* you more freely.

Circle or underline any key words or phrases you *See*:

For by grace you have been saved through faith. And this is not your own doing; it is the gift of God, not a result of works, so that no one may boast. For we are his workmanship, created in Christ Jesus for good works, which God prepared beforehand, that we should walk in them. (Ephesians 2:8-10)

Savor these truths in prayer for yourself and others:

Father, thank you that salvation is a gift. Thank you that it is not based on our good works, but on Jesus' perfect work on the cross. I pray that you would give _____ and me faith to trust you alone for our salvation. Give us your abiding peace that comes from knowing your unconditional acceptance, which you displayed in Jesus' death, burial, and resurrection. Cause us to know how amazingly special we are as your workmanship. Help us to understand and pursue the unique purposes you have prepared for us as your children in Christ. Cause our good works to be a result of our relationship with you, not a means to gain a relationship with you. For your glory and our good, in the precious name of Christ, amen.

Write down any thoughts you may want to *Share*:

DAY NINE // WISDOM

Father, open my eyes that I might *see* you more clearly, *savor* you more fully, and *share* you more freely.

Circle or underline any key words or phrases you *See*:

And he said to man, "Behold, the fear of the Lord, that is wisdom, and to turn away from evil is understanding." (Job 28:28)
The fear of the Lord is the beginning of wisdom; all those who practice it have a good understanding. His praise endures forever! (Psalm 111:10)

Savor these truths in prayer for yourself and others:

Father, you are wise and wonderful in all you are and do. I pray today that _____ and I would fear you in a way that matches your worth. Cause us to see you and ourselves accurately, which produces in us a fear of you that is full of deep respect, honor, and adoration. Create in us a humble dependence on you for all things. Give us deep satisfaction and joy in turning away from evil in both small and big things. Cause our hearts to be filled with insight and understanding concerning the pursuit of the paths of righteousness. Remove the obstacles that blind and deceive us from recognizing your perfect and sovereign work in this world. Make our hearts overflow with praise and thankfulness for all your goodness in our lives. Strengthen us in our ability to help others see your greatness. For your glory and our good, in Jesus' all-wise and wonderful name, amen.

Write down any thoughts you may want to *Share*:

DAY TEN // LOVE

Father, open my eyes that I might *see* you more clearly, *savor* you more fully, and *share* you more freely.

Circle or underline any key words or phrases you *See*:

And he said to him, "You shall love the Lord your God with all your heart and with all your soul and with all your mind. This is the great and first commandment. And a second is like it: You shall love your neighbor as yourself. On these two commandments depend all the Law and the Prophets." (Matthew 22:37-40)

Savor these truths in prayer for yourself and others:

Father, thank you that your greatest command is for our greatest good. I pray that _____ and I would seek to love you with all of our hearts, souls, and minds. Establish yourself as the love of our lives in these formative years. Help us to learn to make decisions in our lives based on the supremacy of your love. Cause us to grow in our ability to know when we are beginning to love other things more than we love you. Give us understanding that our deepest desires can only be satisfied by loving you in all we say, think, and do. Give us an incredible desire and will to love others as we love ourselves. Help us to have a keen sensitivity to the needs of those around us and a willingness to meet those needs. Let our lives be a constant demonstration of your love to the world. For your glory and our good, in the wonderful name of Jesus, amen.

Write down any thoughts you may want to *Share*:

DAY ELEVEN // FAITH

Father, open my eyes that I might *see* you more clearly, *savor* you more fully, and *share* you more freely.

Circle or underline any key words or phrases you *See*:

I know that you can do all things, and that no purpose of yours can be thwarted. (Job 42:2)

Ah, Lord GOD! It is you who have made the heavens and the earth by your great power and by your outstretched arm! Nothing is too hard for you... "Behold, I am the LORD, the God of all flesh. Is anything too hard for me?" (Jeremiah 32:17, 27)

Savor these truths in prayer for yourself and others:

Father, life is filled with challenges and limitations that whisper and sometimes even shout at us saying we are not enough, and yet we rest in knowing that you are more than enough for everything we face in this life. I pray for _____ and myself today, that you would give us faith in your ability to do all things. Help us to believe that there is no purpose of yours that can be thwarted. Help us learn the great stories in your Word that show your faithfulness in difficult times. When we face difficult times, remind us that nothing is too hard for you. Assure us that you work everything for the good of those who love you, so that we might be conformed into the image of your Son. May you be praised forever! In Jesus' name, amen.

Write down any thoughts you may want to *Share*:

DAY TWELVE // PURITY

Father, open my eyes that I might *see* you more clearly, *savor* you more fully, and *share* you more freely.

Circle or underline any key words or phrases you *See:*

I have made a covenant with my eyes; how then could I gaze at a virgin? (Job 31:1)
Sheol and Abaddon are never satisfied, and never satisfied are the eyes of man. (Proverbs 27:20)

Savor these truths in prayer for yourself and others:

Father, I pray for _____ and myself today. I ask that you would make us alert to the people, places, and things that we look upon. Help us to be like Job and make a covenant with our eyes, guarding our gaze and not looking at others inappropriately. Help us to diligently seek purity. Help us to understand that our purity can be fueled or foiled by the direction of our gaze. Protect us from the futility of trying to be satisfied by what we see. The eyes of man cannot be satisfied apart from you. You alone can create in us a satisfaction that supersedes all other lures or lusts that come before our eyes. For your glory and our good, in Jesus' name, amen.

Write down any thoughts you may want to *Share:*

DAY THIRTEEN // SPEECH

Father, open my eyes that I might *see* you more clearly, *savor* you more fully, and *share* you more freely.

Circle or underline any key words or phrases you *See*:

When words are many, transgression is not lacking, but whoever restrains his lips is prudent. (Proverbs 10:19)
There is one whose rash words are like sword thrusts, but the tongue of the wise brings healing. Truthful lips endure forever, but a lying tongue is but for a moment. (Proverbs 12:18-19)

Savor these truths in prayer for yourself and others:

Father, thank you for giving the gift of language and the ability to express ourselves with words. I pray you would bless _____ and me with your wisdom and favor so we can learn to use our words well. Give us wisdom on when to speak and when to keep silent. Protect us from being reckless with our speech and using rash words that damage and destroy. Give us courage to stand up for those who are being verbally bullied. Cause us to grow in your wisdom so that our words would bring healing everywhere we go. Give us a courageous commitment to always speak the truth in love. Help us to know that a lying tongue always comes to an undesirable end. Cause us to be known for the kindness and encouragement in our words. For your glory and our good. In Jesus' name, amen.

Write down any thoughts you may want to *Share*:

DAY FOURTEEN // CONDUCT

Father, open my eyes that I might *see* you more clearly, *savor* you more fully, and *share* you more freely.

Circle or underline any key words or phrases you *See*:

"This Book of the Law shall not depart from your mouth, but you shall meditate on it day and night, so that you may be careful to do according to all that is written in it. For then you will make your way prosperous, and then you will have good success. Have I not commanded you? Be strong and courageous. Do not be frightened, and do not be dismayed, for the LORD your God is with you wherever you go." (Joshua 1:8-9)

Savor these truths in prayer for yourself and others:

Father, I praise you and thank you for the promises in your Word. I pray that _____ and I would take hold of your Word with all our hearts and minds. Give us a craving for your Word that causes us to read, memorize, and meditate on it day and night. Cause us to care about all that you command and be quick to obey you out of a heart of love for you, knowing your promises of goodness will follow. Create in us a courageous and strong resolve to pursue all that you desire for us. Don't let fear cause us to falter. Fill us with faith to believe we can follow you anywhere you command. Give us a sense of your powerful presence to strengthen us to pursue your purposes with courage. For your glory and our good, in Jesus' name, amen.

Write down any thoughts you may want to *Share*:

NOTES

My daughter jokes about how she loves to run short distances at a long distance pace. I laugh every time she says it because I identify with it so much. I wonder if we could benefit by applying my daughter's running approach to our prayers. Here is what I mean: Even though they are short prayers, it doesn't mean you should speed through them. Pace yourself. You can even think of it as a prayer stroll. As you are praying, find a word, phrase, or sentence and linger over it for a little while. Don't feel the need to rush to the next sentence. Let God help you savor the elements of each passage and prayer long into the day. Enjoy your stroll.

....

DAY FIFTEEN // FAVOR

Father, open my eyes that I might *see* you more clearly, *savor* you more fully, and *share* you more freely.

Circle or underline any key words or phrases you *See*:

Let not steadfast love and faithfulness forsake you; bind them around your neck; write them on the tablet of your heart. So you will find favor and good success in the sight of God and man. (Proverbs 3:3-4)

Savor these truths in prayer for yourself and others:

Father, I pray for _____ and myself, that you would lavish us with your favor today. Help us to sense your steadfast love and faithfulness as we go about our day. Cause us to see your goodness by how you have loved and cared for us. Give us opportunities to help others know and experience your love and faithfulness today. May our lives be so clearly marked by your love and faithfulness that favor and success would be our constant companions. Cause us to feel your hand of favor on our lives and remind us that where we go, your favor goes with us. For your glory and our good, in Jesus' name, amen.

Write down any thoughts you may want to *Share*:

DAY SIXTEEN // WISDOM

Father, open my eyes that I might *see* you more clearly, *savor* you more fully, and *share* you more freely.

Circle or underline any key words or phrases you *See*:

For the LORD gives wisdom; from his mouth come knowledge and understanding; he stores up sound wisdom for the upright... (Proverbs 2:6-7)
Blessed is the one who finds wisdom, and the one who gets understanding... (Proverbs 3:13)

Savor these truths in prayer for yourself and others:

Father, I pray that you would create in _____ and me a longing for you and your wisdom. I pray that you would give us eyes to see, ears to hear, and hearts to understand the wisdom found in your Word! Protect us from becoming foolish and proud and from not understanding the truth of how limited our knowledge and understanding really is. Cause us to humbly treasure the truth of your wisdom. Bless us in our relationship with you as we taste the sweetness of your wisdom. Create in us a deep understanding about life, which enables us to be fountains of wise counsel to our friends. Make sharing about you and your wisdom as natural as breathing for us. For your glory and our good, in Jesus' name, amen.

Write down any thoughts you may want to *Share*:

DAY SEVENTEEN // LOVE

Father, open my eyes that I might *see* you more clearly, *savor* you more fully, and *share* you more freely.

Circle or underline any key words or phrases you *See*:

For as high as the heavens are above the earth, so great is his steadfast love toward those who fear him; as far as the east is from the west, so far does he remove our transgressions from us. (Psalm 103:11-12)

Savor these truths in prayer for yourself and others:

Father, I pray that _____ and I would gain an ever-growing understanding that your love is great toward those who fear you! Stir up within us a sense of awe and respect for you that is unquenchable. Cause us to feel the vastness of your love for us that stretches to the highest heavens as we look at the daytime sky and the night's starry host. Thank you that your love and forgiveness are perfect and complete. Let us feel the freedom of your complete and unending forgiveness through Jesus and his sacrifice every single day. Help us to be open and available to show your love and forgiveness in any way that we can. For your glory and our good, in Jesus' name, amen.

Write down any thoughts you may want to *Share*:

DAY EIGHTEEN // FAITH

Father, open my eyes that I might *see* you more clearly, *savor* you more fully, and *share* you more freely.

Circle or underline any key words or phrases you *See*:

And those who know your name put their trust in you, for you, O LORD, have not forsaken those who seek you. (Psalm 9:10)
Some trust in chariots and some in horses, but we trust in the name of the LORD our God. (Psalm 20:7)

Savor these truths in prayer for yourself and others:

Father, thank you for all of your promises in your Word. They are testaments of your faithfulness in our lives. I pray for _____ and myself, that we would know your character, causing our hearts to grow strong in faith and trust in your promises. Create in us confidence that your name represents all authority, power, and greatness. Help our hearts to be receptive to you as our Creator, Sustainer, Provider, Healer, and Redeemer. Help us to feel secure and safe in knowing that you will never forsake us. You are the Prince of Peace, so anoint us with your perfect peace. You are the King of Kings, so reign over us in all of your goodness. You are the Great I Am, so give us faith to trust you for all we need. For your glory and our good, in Jesus' name, amen.

Write down any thoughts you may want to *Share*:

DAY NINETEEN // PURITY

Father, open my eyes that I might *see* you more clearly, *savor* you more fully, and *share* you more freely.

Circle or underline any key words or phrases you *See*:

Blessed are the pure in heart, for they shall see God.
(Matthew 5:8)

Savor these truths in prayer for yourself and others:

Father, thank you for this day that you have ordained for me and _____. I pray for our happiness today. Jesus said that blessed are the pure in heart for they shall see God. Give us uncontainable joy in you. Don't let us miss the wonder and joy of seeing you because we settled for some false promise of pleasure elsewhere. Give us a magnificent vision of your greatness so that those empty promises would be powerless in our hearts. It is by your Spirit that we are empowered to walk in purity. Fill us with your Spirit today. Cause the joy from seeing your magnificence to overflow in blessing and purity to those around us. For your glory and our good, in Jesus' name, amen.

Write down any thoughts you may want to *Share*:

DAY TWENTY // SPEECH

Father, open my eyes that I might *see* you more clearly, *savor* you more fully, and *share* you more freely.

Circle or underline any key words or phrases you *See*:

The wise of heart is called discerning, and sweetness of speech increases persuasiveness. Good sense is a foundation of life to him who has it, but the instruction of fools is folly. The heart of the wise makes his speech judicious and adds persuasiveness to his lips. Gracious words are like a honeycomb, sweetness to the soul and health to the body. (Proverbs 16:21-24)

Savor these truths in prayer for yourself and others:

Father, your Word tells us that out of the heart the mouth speaks and that a wise heart guides our speech to make a difference for good. I pray that _____ and I would have hearts that are fueled by your wisdom so that our speech would be sweet and persuasive. May your hand of favor be so clearly on our lives that our speech is powerfully discerning. Help our friends to also have hearts that are rooted in wisdom so that we can encourage and correct each other along the way. Grant that our words would be filled with grace so that they may give comfort to the soul and body. For your glory and our good, in Jesus' name, amen.

Write down any thoughts you may want to *Share*:

DAY TWENTY-ONE // CONDUCT

Father, open my eyes that I might *see* you more clearly, *savor* you more fully, and *share* you more freely.

Circle or underline any key words or phrases you *See*:

Good and upright is the LORD; therefore he instructs sinners in the way. He leads the humble in what is right, and teaches the humble his way. All the paths of the LORD are steadfast love and faithfulness, for those who keep his covenant and his testimonies. (Psalm 25:8-10)

Savor these truths in prayer for yourself and others:

Father, thank you that you are good and upright in all you do. Thank you for correcting us when we stray from your truth and instructing us in the way we should go. I pray that you would create in _____ and me humble hearts that are teachable and responsive to all of your instruction and purposes. Help us understand that you lead the humble in all that is right and that you teach them to live in your ways. Give us joy in obeying your Word that flows from a growing conviction that all your paths are paved with steadfast love and faithfulness. Cause us to be relentless in pursuing your paths of steadfast love and faithfulness. Help us to make friends who help us in our pursuit of your purposes. Make your truth our treasure. For your glory and our good, in Jesus' name, amen.

Write down any thoughts you may want to *Share*:

NOTES

Praying for your friends by yourself is invigorating, but I want to encourage you to consider widening your circle. Find a friend who is also a Prayer Champion and pray together for your peers perhaps once a week. If that's too big of a commitment for you, consider doing it once a month. You will find that praying this Prayer Guide with someone is easy and incredibly encouraging. You may find it so encouraging that you create a Prayer Champions' prayer group to strengthen your efforts of interceding for your generation!

For where two or three are gathered in my name, there I am among them. (Matthew 18:20)

....

DAY TWENTY-TWO // FAVOR

Father, open my eyes that I might *see* you more clearly, *savor* you more fully, and *share* you more freely.

Circle or underline any key words or phrases you *See*:

What do you have that you did not receive? If then you received it, why do you boast as if you did not receive it? (1 Corinthians 4:7)
    ...since he himself gives to all mankind life and breath and everything... "in him we live and move and have our being." (Acts 17:25, 28)

Savor these truths in prayer for yourself and others:

Father, every breath is a gift of your grace and favor. I thank you for giving _____ and me life and breath and all things. Show us your sustaining favor that makes it possible for us to live and move and have our being. Keep us from taking your enduring goodness and favor for granted. Give us eyes to see your sustaining favor and create genuine delight in our hearts today for each breath. Make our hearts full with thanksgiving for the gift of your gracious favor. For your glory and our good, in the all-sustaining name of Jesus, amen.

Write down any thoughts you may want to *Share*:

DAY TWENTY-THREE // WISDOM

Father, open my eyes that I might *see* you more clearly, *savor* you more fully, and *share* you more freely.

Circle or underline any key words or phrases you *See*:

The words of the wise are like goads, and like nails firmly fixed are the collected sayings; they are given by one Shepherd. My son, beware of anything beyond these. Of making many books there is no end, and much study is a weariness of the flesh. The end of the matter; all has been heard. Fear God and keep his commandments, for this is the whole duty of man. For God will bring every deed into judgment, with every secret thing, whether good or evil. (Ecclesiastes 12:11-14)

Savor these truths in prayer for yourself and others:

Father, thank you for reminding us that wisdom comes from you, the Great Shepherd. I pray that _____ and I would have an exceptional desire to want to know first and foremost what you think and say in your Word about how we should live. Help us wade deeply into the Biblical proverbs and the parables of Jesus, letting the truths soak thoroughly into our lives. Cause our understanding of life and how it works to grow deep and wide so that we would become incredible influencers for your purposes in this world. Strengthen us by the power of your Spirit to honor and obey you in all things, knowing that we're ultimately accountable to you. For your glory and our good, in Jesus' name, amen.

Write down any thoughts you may want to *Share*:

DAY TWENTY-FOUR // LOVE

Father, open my eyes that I might *see* you more clearly, *savor* you more fully, and *share* you more freely.

Circle or underline any key words or phrases you *See*:

For the love of money is a root of all kinds of evils. It is through this craving that some have wandered away from the faith and pierced themselves with many pangs. (1 Timothy 6:10)

Keep your life free from love of money, and be content with what you have, for he has said, "I will never leave you nor forsake you." So we can confidently say, "The Lord is my helper; I will not fear; what can man do to me?" (Hebrews 13:5-6)

Savor these truths in prayer for yourself and others:

Father, as I pray for _____ and myself today, I long for us to have our hearts captured by you and your love. So many things can steal our affections—the love of money being one of the most significant and potentially tragic. Your Word says that the love of money is the root of all kinds of evils. Protect us from ever allowing the love of money and all the material things it can buy to be the driving force of our lives. Help us understand that money provides a sense of security, which can tempt us to hope in money rather than your loving relationship with us. Give us confidence that you are our helper; there is no need to fear because you will never leave or forsake us. For your glory and our good, in Jesus' name, amen.

Write down any thoughts you may want to *Share*:

DAY TWENTY-FIVE // FAITH

Father, open my eyes that I might *see* you more clearly, *savor* you more fully, and *share* you more freely.

Circle or underline any key words or phrases you *See:*

The fear of man lays a snare, but whoever trusts in the Lord is safe. (Proverbs 29:25)

Savor these truths in prayer for yourself and others:

Father, I praise you today that you are great and glorious and worthy of all our trust. We do not need to be afraid and yet fear so often grips our hearts. I pray that you would help _____ and me to see your trustworthiness and learn to rest in your goodness. Help us not to be afraid of what other people think of us. Set us free from the snares and limitations that come from giving others too big of a place in our hearts and minds. Instead, cause our hearts to grow big in believing that you are safe and good and that you alone can set us free from fearing others. Cause our trust in you to guide what we think, say, and do today. For your glory and our good, in Jesus' name, amen.

Write down any thoughts you may want to *Share:*

DAY TWENTY-SIX // PURITY

Father, open my eyes that I might *see* you more clearly, *savor* you more fully, and *share* you more freely.

Circle or underline any key words or phrases you *See*:

Keep your heart with all vigilance, for from it flow the springs of life. (Proverbs 4:23)

And he said, "What comes out of a person is what defiles him. For from within, out of the heart of man, come evil thoughts, sexual immorality, theft, murder, adultery, coveting, wickedness, deceit, sensuality, envy, slander, pride, foolishness. All these evil things come from within, and they defile a person." (Mark 7:20-23)

Savor these truths in prayer for yourself and others:

Father, in our pursuit of following you in faithfulness and becoming like you in holiness, we realize that some actions are more important than others. Guarding our hearts is one of those vital acts. I pray that _____ and I would exercise vigilance in guarding our hearts by the power of your Spirit. Help us to see the places where we need to protect our hearts better. Help us to find friends that will strengthen our resolve to guard our hearts. Cause us to see with clarity the disappointing consequences of living with an unguarded heart. Fill us with your Spirit so that rivers of living water will flow out of us. For your glory and our good, in Jesus' name, amen.

Write down any thoughts you may want to *Share*:

DAY TWENTY-SEVEN // SPEECH

Father, open my eyes that I might *see* you more clearly, *savor* you more fully, and *share* you more freely.

Circle or underline any key words or phrases you *See*:

A soft answer turns away wrath, but a harsh word stirs up anger. The tongue of the wise commends knowledge, but the mouths of fools pour out folly...A gentle tongue is a tree of life, but perverseness in it breaks the spirit. (Proverbs 15:1-2, 4)

Savor these truths in prayer for yourself and others:

Father, thank you for the power of soft and gentle speech. I pray that you would provide _____ and me with people who would lavish us with the goodness of soft and gentle speech. In the same way I pray that we would be generous in offering up words that are soft and gentle to others. Cause the fruit of our words to be a tree of life, turning away wrath and anger. Let wisdom flow from our lips, commending knowledge that is life-giving to all who hear. Protect us from giving or receiving harsh words that stir up anger or hate. Give us the ability to graciously change the subject when perverse speech breaks out around us. Do not let evil and harsh words be used to harm us in any way. Help us to embrace your truth so we can overcome any false words directed toward us. For your glory and our good, in Jesus' name, amen.

Write down any thoughts you may want to *Share*:

DAY TWENTY-EIGHT // CONDUCT

Father, open my eyes that I might *see* you more clearly, *savor* you more fully, and *share* you more freely.

Circle or underline any key words or phrases you *See:*

Be appalled, O heavens, at this; be shocked, be utterly desolate, declares the LORD, for my people have committed two evils: they have forsaken me, the fountain of living waters, and hewed out cisterns for themselves, broken cisterns that can hold no water. (Jeremiah 2:12-13)

Savor these truths in prayer for yourself and others:

Father, thank you that you are the fountain of living waters and the only place we can be perfectly satisfied. I pray that _____ and I would believe fully that you are enough to satisfy our hearts. Make us aware of even the slightest tendency to turn away from you to find happiness somewhere else. Cause us to see and understand how appalling and shocking it is for your children to turn away from you to find life. Help us to flee the futility of trying to find happiness through our own devices. Forgive us when we think about or pursue you in a casual way. Create in us a craving for you and your ways that surpasses every promise of pleasure in other things. Help those around us to turn away from their futile ways and find fullness of joy in you. For your glory and our good, in Jesus' name, amen.

Write down any thoughts you may want to *Share:*

NOTES

Before God enables his people to bring in a harvest, he pours out a Spirit of prayer upon them. The surest sign that God is about to send power upon us is a great movement of prayer in our midst. —John Piper

....

DAY TWENTY-NINE // FAVOR

Father, open my eyes that I might *see* you more clearly, *savor* you more fully, and *share* you more freely.

Circle or underline any key words or phrases you *See*:

My son, do not forget my teaching, but let your heart keep my commandments, for length of days and years of life and peace they will add to you. Let not steadfast love and faithfulness forsake you; bind them around your neck; write them on the tablet of your heart. So you will find favor and good success in the sight of God and man. (Proverbs 3:1-4)

Savor these truths in prayer for yourself and others:

Father, I pray for _____ and myself today, that you would bring to mind your Word and give us hearts that treasure your commands. Cause us to embrace the instruction for daily guidance, resulting in long and peace-filled lives. Help us keep your steadfast love and faithfulness in the forefront of our minds. Give us creativity in how we seek to live lives of love and faithfulness. Help us memorize and enjoy your love and faithfulness on a daily basis. Cause us to find favor and good success with you and man. Give us eyes to see your hand of favor in our lives and cause our hearts to grow big in love and faithfulness toward you and others. For your glory and our good, in Jesus' name, amen.

Write down any thoughts you may want to *Share*:

DAY THIRTY // WISDOM

Father, open my eyes that I might *see* you more clearly, *savor* you more fully, and *share* you more freely.

Circle or underline any key words or phrases you *See*:

Blessed is the one who finds wisdom, and the one who gets understanding, for the gain from her is better than gain from silver and her profit better than gold. She is more precious than jewels, and nothing you desire can compare with her. Long life is in her right hand; in her left hand are riches and honor. Her ways are ways of pleasantness, and all her paths are peace. She is a tree of life to those who lay hold of her; those who hold her fast are called blessed. (Proverbs 3:13-18)

Savor these truths in prayer for yourself and others:

Father, I pray for _____ and myself today, that we would know the blessing of finding wisdom and understanding. Give us strong desires for you that propel us toward seeking wisdom and understanding. Give us taste buds so we may savor the treasures of a life that are found in your magnificent wisdom and understanding. May long life, riches, honor, and great joy be ours as we follow your path of wisdom leading to peace and pleasantness. Cause our paths to lead to the tree of life, most specifically to the cross of Christ. It was your wisdom that made life possible in Jesus. Cause our hearts to pursue your wisdom above all else. For your glory and our good, in Jesus' name, amen.

Write down any thoughts you may want to *Share*:

DAY THIRTY-ONE // LOVE

Father, open my eyes that I might *see* you more clearly, *savor* you more fully, and *share* you more freely.

Circle or underline any key words or phrases you *See*:

For this reason I bow my knees before the Father, from whom every family in heaven and on earth is named, that according to the riches of his glory he may grant you to be strengthened with power through his Spirit in your inner being, so that Christ may dwell in your hearts through faith—that you, being rooted and grounded in love, may have strength to comprehend with all the saints what is the breadth and length and height and depth, and to know the love of Christ that surpasses knowledge, that you may be filled with all the fullness of God. (Ephesians 3:14-19)

Savor these truths in prayer for yourself and others:

Father, it is by your wisdom that the earth was founded and the heavens established, and for that we praise your name. I pray that _____ and I would see the goodness of your provision in all of creation. Cause us to learn to savor the greatness of your wisdom as we touch a blade of grass or see the stars above. May our hearts be encouraged by your sovereignty every time a raindrop splashes on our faces. Make us tenacious in seeing the preciousness of sound wisdom and discretion in everyday life. Surround us with people who walk in your wisdom and whose lives bear the fruit of your favor. Give us security, stability, peace, and sweetness of sleep because of it. For your glory and our good, in Jesus' name, amen.

Write down any thoughts you may want to *Share*:

PART FOUR

....

PRAYING FOR THE LOST

You have just completed seven weeks of praying through The 7 Essentials for you and your peers! Hopefully you are getting the hang of praying Scripture as a vital way to strengthen your prayer life. Praying for others who know Christ is a crucial part of helping them become transformed into his image as God intends them to be. As awesome as it is to pray for other followers of Christ, it is absolutely crucial for us to learn how to pray for those who don't know him personally. God uses our prayers as one of the means of drawing people to himself. The following section is designed to equip you to begin praying effectively for those in your world who do not yet know Christ. I love the zing of clarity that John Piper shares in his book about missions, *Let the Nations Be Glad:*

> Missions is not the ultimate goal of the church. Worship is. Missions exists because worship doesn't. Worship is ultimate, not missions, because God is ultimate, not man. When this age is over, and the countless millions of the redeemed fall on their faces before the throne of God, missions will be no more. It is a temporary necessity. But worship abides forever.

141

Wow! Piper uses the term "missions," but he could have just as easily said "evangelism"—the principle is the same. Missions or evangelism is not the ultimate goal, but it is a means to helping as many people as we can to join us in what we were created for. We pray and share the Gospel with those who don't know Christ so that they can enjoy the unceasing pleasure of his magnificence for eternity. So how can we pray in a way that will help our friends and peers see and savor the beauty of Jesus personally?

Three Starter Strategies for Praying for the Lost

Strategy One: Know the Gospel

A great place to start is making sure you understand the key components of the Gospel and beginning to pray through each one of these components for your friends. There are lots of great resources available to help you understand the Gospel more fully and share it with your friends. Two that I want to specifically recommend are Everystudent.com and Dare 2 Share. Everystudent.com's motto is "A Safe Place to Explore Questions About Life and God" and it serves as just that. Dare 2 Share, a ministry that equips students to share their faith, has a wealth of great resources on their website (www.dare2share.org) and mobile apps, which are incredibly helpful in understanding and sharing the Gospel. Their Life in 6 Words G.O.S.P.E.L. approach has helped me and countless others gain understanding in the straightforward message of the Gospel. Lastly, Greg Stier, president of Dare 2 Share, has written a 40-day devotional that is very helpful in understanding the Gospel more fully. Take a minute to read over the Life in 6 Words G.O.S.P.E.L. listed below:

- GOD created us to be with Him.
- OUR sins separate us from God.

- SINS cannot be removed by good deeds.
- PAYING the price for sin, Jesus died and rose again.
- EVERYONE who trusts in Him alone has eternal life.
- LIFE with Jesus starts now and lasts forever.[1]

I encourage you to hover over each aspect of the G.O.S.P.E.L. Let each truth sink deeply into your heart and mind so that you feel the weight of it: the God who created you to be with him; the tragedy of how our sin separates us from God; the hopelessness of trying to be good enough to remove your sin; the amazing love and sacrifice of Jesus who paid the price for our sin by his death and resurrection; the inexpressible joy that all who trust in Jesus for salvation have eternal life; the unwavering hope that life with Jesus starts the moment you place your trust in him and never ends. Memorize this acrostic and begin to pray through it for others so that they would know and embrace the Gospel.

If this is News to You...

Perhaps as you have been reading and praying through this book you have come to realize that you have never trusted in Jesus alone for your salvation. You may have been connected to a church for some time, but Christ has never become the treasure and hope of your life like the story in Matthew 13:44. It is a brief but powerful story of a man who is traveling and comes upon a treasure in a field. He realizes he has stumbled upon what he has been looking for all his life. He buries it in a field and sells everything he has to buy the field and keep the treasure. Jesus is the treasure and he is worth everything we could ever give to have him as our Lord and Savior! That realization is a gift from God. You can embrace Jesus as your treasure through prayer right now. Below is a prayer that

[1] ©Dare 2 Share. www.dare2share.org. Used by permission.

can help you invite Jesus into your life as your Lord and Savior. The exact words of the prayer are not as important as the intentions of your heart. God knows you better than anyone and longs for you to be in relationship with him. The prayer is offered to help you launch into the most important relationship you will ever have:

Dear Jesus, I want to know you personally. I want you to come into my life and become my greatest treasure. I know my sins have separated me from you. Thank you for dying for me and forgiving my sins to bring me into relationship with God. I trust and follow you now as my Lord and Savior. Help me by the power of your Holy Spirit to become the person you created me to be. In your name, amen.

If you just prayed the above prayer or your own prayer to invite Jesus to be your Lord and Savior, Congratulations!! This is the most important decision you will ever make. Now it is time to share the news. I encourage you to let your ministry, pastor, parents, and friends know about your decision and let them join in the celebration. I would also love to join in the celebration. Send me an email (tony@theyouthnetwork) and let me know the good news!

Strategy Two: Prepare the Soil

The Bible is a story of redemption from the first pages of Genesis to the end of Revelation. God gives us behind-the-scenes sneak peeks throughout the Bible into how he redeems people and draws them to himself. The five passages starting on the next page are some that I've come across over the years that are instrumental in how I pray for those who do not yet have a relationship with Jesus Christ. This is definitely not a complete list of passages you could pray to prepare the way for your friends to trust Christ, but I think it will help you get started. Feel free to add to them and create your own more extensive list, as you pray for those in your life who don't know Christ.

Strategy Three: Pray The 7 Essentials with a Salvation Slant

This third strategy is simple. Use the entire Prayer Guide as an effective daily tool in praying for those in your world who don't know Christ. The prayers are already deeply rooted in the Gospel and our need for Christ in all things, so praying through The 7 Essentials for your friends who don't know Christ will only require you to adjust your thinking a little. Praying for your friends' and peers' salvation is one of the most important things we can do for them. It is an amazing gift from God that we get to help them enter into a personal relationship with the creator and sustainer of the universe.

Pray on!

PREPARING THE SOIL // PRAYING FOR YOUR FRIENDS TO KNOW CHRIST

Becoming a follower of Christ is the single greatest thing that can ever happen to anyone at any time. It is a great privilege to plead with God to do his work: drawing people to himself and making them alive by shining the light of the greatness of Christ in their hearts as referenced below in 2 Corinthians 4:4-6. May God be pleased to use our prayers and lives to bring our peers to himself.

In their case the god of this world has blinded the minds of the unbelievers, to keep them from seeing the light of the gospel of the glory of Christ, who is the image of God. For what we proclaim is not ourselves. But Jesus Christ as Lord, with ourselves as your servants for Jesus' sake. For God, who said, "Let light shine out of darkness," has shone in our hearts to give the light of the knowledge of the glory of God in the face of Jesus Christ (2 Corinthians 4:4-6).

No one can come to me unless the Father who sent me draws him. And I will raise him up on the last day (John 6:44).

1 // GIVE THEM EYES TO SEE

Father, open my eyes that I might *see* you more clearly, *savor* you more fully, and *share* you more freely.

Circle or underline any key words or phrases you *See*:

In their case the god of this world has blinded the minds of the unbelievers, to keep them from seeing the light of the gospel of the glory of Christ, who is the image of God. For what we proclaim is not ourselves, but Jesus Christ as Lord, with ourselves as your servants for Jesus' sake. For God, who said, "Let light shine out of darkness," has shone in our hearts to give the light of the knowledge of the glory of God in the face of Jesus Christ. (2 Corinthians 4:4-6)

Savor these truths in prayer:

Father, I ask that you would thwart the efforts of the god of this world to blind my friends from your greatness. Remove the blinders from their minds and give them the ability to see the full light of the Gospel of Christ. Shine in their hearts the knowledge of the glory of God through the face of Jesus Christ. Cause all of their senses to be saturated by the wonders of Jesus Christ so they would turn to him for eternal life. Cause their hearts and minds to find enormous delight in every new thing they learn about your greatness. For your glory and their good, in Jesus name, amen.

Write down any thoughts you may want to *Share*:

2 // DRAW THEM

Father, open my eyes that I might *see* you more clearly, *savor* you more fully, and *share* you more freely.

Circle or underline any key words or phrases you *See*:

No one can come to me unless the Father who sent me draws him. And I will raise him up on the last day. It is written in the Prophets, 'And they will all be taught by God.' Everyone who has heard and learned from the Father comes to me... Truly, truly, I say to you, whoever believes has eternal life." (John 6:44-45, 47)

Savor these truths in prayer:

Father, draw my friends to yourself. Be the all-powerful magnetic force that pulls them into relationship with you. Cause them to desire more out of this life than what they can see. Create in them a desire for a relationship with you. Teach my friends truth in their hearts. Give them ears to hear and understand what you want them to know so they will believe and have eternal life. May these prayers be used to draw them to yourself. For your glory and their good, in Jesus' name, amen.

Write down any thoughts you may want to *Share*:

3 // MAKE THEM ALIVE

Father, open my eyes that I might *see* you more clearly, *savor* you more fully, and *share* you more freely.

Circle or underline any key words or phrases you *See*:

And you were dead in the trespasses and sins...But God, being rich in mercy, because of the great love with which he loved us, even when we were dead in our trespasses, made us alive together with Christ—by grace you have been saved... (Ephesians 2:1, 4-5)

Savor these truths in prayer:

Father, those who don't know you are spiritually dead. They need you to make them alive. In your abundant mercy make them alive with Christ. I pray you will break the hold of spiritual death and give them life by your matchless grace. There is no hope apart from your grace that moves in and brings to life the spiritually dead. Use your Word and Spirit to awaken them. You are the only one who can give them life and yet you use people like me to share your Word and to plead their case before your throne. Empower me to stay the course in caring for my friends through prayer and actions. For your glory and their good, in Jesus' name, amen.

Write down any thoughts you may want to *Share*:

4 // GIVE THEM THE GIFT OF FAITH

Father, open my eyes that I might *see* you more clearly, *savor* you more fully, and *share* you more freely.

Circle or underline any key words or phrases you *See*:

For by grace you have been saved through faith. And this is not your own doing; it is the gift of God, not a result of works, so that no one may boast. (Ephesians 2:8-9)

So faith comes from hearing, and hearing through the word of Christ. (Romans 10:17)

And without faith it is impossible to please him, for whoever would draw near to God must believe that he exists and that he rewards those who seek him. (Hebrews 11:6)

Whoever believes in the Son has eternal life; whoever does not obey the Son shall not see life, but the wrath of God remains on him. (John 3:36)

Savor these truths in prayer:

Father, my friends need an outpouring of your lavish grace so that they can be saved through faith. Give them faith to believe that there isn't anything better than knowing Jesus Christ personally. Help them to realize how lost they are without you, and that without faith they have no hope of pleasing you. Give them ears to hear the truth from your word about Christ and believe in him with all their hearts and minds. Help them to know that their relationship with you is not based on their performance, but on you giving your son to die for our sins. Jesus the righteous one gave his life for the unrighteous ones in order to bring us to God. Remove all the obstacles to their believing so they can be in relationship with you forever. For your glory and their good, in Jesus' name, amen.

Write down any thoughts you may want to *Share*:

5 // SHOW THEM KINDNESS

Father, open my eyes that I might *see* you more clearly, *savor* you more fully, and *share* you more freely.

Circle or underline any key words or phrases you *See*:

Or do you presume on the riches of his kindness and forbearance and patience, not knowing that God's kindness is meant to lead you to repentance?" (Romans 2:4)

Savor these truths in prayer:

Father, you are so good and glorious in all that you do. The riches of your kindness and patience are lavished on us every day of our lives, and yet we are often blind to your gifts. I pray you will give my friends eyes to see your kindness toward them today. As you help them see the magnitude of your kindness and patience, I pray you would soften their hearts toward you. Cause your kindness to have its way in their hearts so they would repent and turn away from trying to find true life outside of you. Help them turn away from fleeting pleasures that can never satisfy and turn towards your Son, who came that they might have life in abundance. For your glory and their good, in Jesus' name, amen.

Write down any thoughts you may want to *Share*:

NOTES

Prompts for Praying for Your School

Praying for your school is not an abstract venture; it is personal because it is made up of people, people who need prayer at every turn. People like you and me who are trying to find their way in life. Every day they are making choices that will impact hundreds if not thousands of lives. Some of these choices and decisions will affect multiple generations to come. Your headmaster, principal, chancellor or dean along with the other administrative leaders and teachers need your prayers. Your fellow students and the support staff, like secretaries and janitorial staff, all need the kind of prayers you have been praying all through this Prayer Guide.

The following prompts fall into 6 categories to help guide you in praying for your school. They are obviously not exhaustive but I pray they are helpful for you as you seek to be tenacious in prayer for your school.

First: Pray for Yourself
Pray for yourself that you would have eyes to see, ears to hear and a heart that understands the needs of those around you like Jesus did. Pray especially to see the disadvantaged, discouraged, isolated and ignored who are on your campus. Ask God to help you live a life that is marked by the call in Micah 6:8 to act justly, love mercy and walk humbly with your God. God calls us as his children to be servants to our schools, and he will awaken us to the needs of those around us when we pray. Pray that God would help you to become more courageous and compassionate so that you can love your campus without fear.

Second: Pray for Christians
Pray for all those in your school who are following Christ, whether students, teachers, staff or administration. All of you are God's representatives on your campus. Pray that the favor of God would cause the beauty, wonder and greatness of Christ to

become their greatest treasure. It is only when Jesus is your greatest treasure that you will be free to boldly love and bless those on your campus. I would encourage you to pray the 7 Essentials for the Christians on your campus, just like you have done throughout this whole Prayer Guide. They need God's Favor, Wisdom, Love, Faith and Purity to speak and live in such a way that brings glory to God and blessing to others.

Third: Pray for non-Christians
Pray for all those in your school who do not know Christ personally, whether students, teachers, staff or administrative leaders. Just like you and me they were created to be in relationship with God the Father. As John 14:6 tells us, it is only through Jesus Christ that they can have the ultimate relationship they were created for. Ask God to give you a relentless passion to see everyone on your campus come to know Christ personally. I encourage you to use the section for praying for the lost on page 141 to help you pray specifically for them.

Fourth: Pray for Protection and Provision
Pray that all that is good and right would flourish at your school and all that is evil and wrong would be thwarted. Pray that God would empower you and other Christians to be filled with the Holy Spirit and bear the fruit of the Spirit. That all of you would be the greatest advocates of love, joy, peace, patience, kindness, goodness, faithfulness, gentleness and self-control on your campus. Pray that you and the other Christians would be extraordinarily courageous to stop acts of injustice and abuse whether it is physical, sexual or emotional. Pray that God would cover your campus with protection from all those who would seek to do violence and cause harm.

Fifth: Pray for Thankfulness
God is at work on your campus through you and the other Christians to advance his purposes and bring glory to himself. Pray that God would give you eyes to see what he is doing on your

campus. Be sure to spend time savoring all that you see God doing at your school. Savor his works with prayers of thankfulness. In 1 Thessalonians 5:18 we are commanded to "Give thanks in all circumstances for this is the will of God in Christ Jesus for you." Give thanks, by name, for those on your campus who are faithfully pursuing Christ. Give thanks for teachers, coaches and other staff who work diligently to help students flourish. Giving thanks in prayer honors God and places us in a posture of joyful dependence upon him as our creator and sustainer. Thankfulness is one of the most powerful means God uses to transform us into His likeness.

Sixth: Share Your Prayer

This final prompt is primarily an encouragement for you to be a catalyst for prayer for your school. Invite your friends to join you in prayer for your school. Gather together with friends to pray. You may even consider buying them one of these Prayer Guides to help them pray. Sometimes a simple gift like that will be just what is needed to help someone grow closer to Jesus through prayer. Another action point would be to talk to your pastor about encouraging your church to pray for your school. Also, if your church is doing the Pray for Me Campaign, invite your Prayer Champions to join you in praying. The last aspect of this prompt is for you to make sure to share what you see God doing on your campus. Take a moment and look back at the SeeSavorShare discipleship process I wrote about on pages 5-10. Sharing what God is doing in your life and on your campus is a key way of sharing your faith with others. These God Stories will provide great encouragement for others and will remind you that God is Real and at work in and through you.

May the Lord in all of His Greatness use your prayers to lavish His goodness on your school.

EPILOGUE

You did it! You've made it to the end of the Pray for Me Prayer Guide! But, the end doesn't have to be the end. My prayer is that you enjoyed the process and will continue to use this Prayer Guide as a source of encouragement to deepen your life with God in prayer. I hope you'll pray these prayers early and often for both yourself and all those who surround your life who need a deep and authentic relationship with Jesus.

I also want you to know that you're not alone. There are students all across America using this very Prayer Guide to pray for themselves and their peers. You are part of a broader community of young people seeking to know Jesus more! I hope that as you continue to experience the adventure of prayer that you will invite others to join you on this journey by sharing this Prayer Guide with your friends. You are making a difference for the Kingdom through your prayers.

Lastly, I want to finish with how I began this book in the dedication.

To You, the Next Generation:

May the magnificence of Jesus capture your hearts daily!
May prayer become as natural and vital for you as breathing!
May you become relentlessly courageous for the cause of Christ!

Tony Souder

WHAT'S NEXT?

As a student, take the next step and become a Movement Champion for the Pray for Me Campaign. You can advance the movement in three strategic ways!

1. **Pray**. Movement Champions pray for the advancement of the Campaign.
2. **Share.** Movement Champions tell others about the Campaign.
3. **Give.** Movement Champions give financially to advance the Campaign.

Become a Movement Champion today!

www.prayformecampaign.com/give